DONALD
DAVIDSON

Donald Davidson in 1965

DONALD DAVIDSON

AN ESSAY ❧ AND A BIBLIOGRAPHY

by Thomas Daniel Young and M. Thomas Inge

VANDERBILT UNIVERSITY PRESS ❧ *Nashville—1965*

Magistro a discipulis

Contents

Illustrations

Acknowledgments

The authors wish to express appreciation to Mr. Donald Davidson for allowing us to use letters, manuscripts, and other documents from his private papers. The four unpublished versions of "Lee in the Mountains" are in Mr. Davidson's possession, and we are particularly grateful to him for permission to reproduce Drafts One and Four and to quote lines and passages from Drafts Two and Three.

We also want to thank Mr. Allen Tate for permission to quote from his letter of January 19, 1934, to Mr. Davidson and to reproduce his comments on Draft Four of "Lee in the Mountains."

The University of Georgia Press has kindly permitted us to use material included in Davidson's *Southern Writers in the Modern World*.

LEE IN THE MOUNTAINS

The Making of a Poem

Donald Davidson spent the college year of 1932–33 in Marshallville, Georgia, the home of his good friend John Donald Wade. For several years Davidson, like some of his fellow Agrarians, had been intensely interested in Southern history, particularly Civil War history.[1] *I'll Take My Stand: The South and the Agrarian Tradition* had been published in 1930 and dedicated to Professor Walter Fleming, an eminent Southern historian. Although Davidson's contribution to that symposium was concerned primarily with the plight of the arts and artists in an industrial society, his interest in the developments of the twentieth century had led him to look carefully at many facets of Southern history. During the spring of 1933, at the home of Andrew Lytle's father in Guntersville, Alabama, he met several of the other contributors to *I'll Take My Stand*. At this meeting Seward Collins, editor and publisher of *The Bookman*, discussed his plans for the *American Review* and indicated that he would welcome contributions from the Agrarians and others of their point of view.[2]

1. During this period, too, Davidson was reading Charles A. Beard's *The Rise of American Civilization* (1927) and F. J. Turner's *The Significance of Sections in American History* (1932), two books that figure prominently in Davidson's study of sectionalism: *The Attack on Leviathan* (Chapel Hill: University of North Carolina Press, 1938).

2. This meeting was a continuation of one that had occurred earlier in

From 1933 to 1936, when the second symposium—*Who Owns America?*—was published, Davidson was advancing on many fronts the primary beliefs that he continues to hold. During these years he presented ordered, cogent arguments in behalf of his Agrarian principles in such divergent publications as *The Southern Review, American Review, Hound and Horn, American Mercury, Virginia Quarterly Review, Progressive Farmer* and several Southern newspapers. While Davidson was preparing these prose essays, he was carrying a full teaching schedule at Vanderbilt University in the regular academic year and at the Bread Loaf School of English of Middlebury College during the summers. One may well wonder, therefore, how there was any time left for poetry.

But 1932–33 was a year of relative leisure. He was free of his teaching and, though he was engaged in correspondence with Collins and his fellow Agrarians, planning for their future association with *American Review*, there was time for reading and writing. He read widely in American history and wrote "Old Black Joe," "Randall, My Son," and "The Running of Streight," three poems that were later to appear in *Lee in the Mountains and Other Poems*. During the winter of 1932 and the early spring of 1933, he composed his essay "Sectionalism in the United States," which appeared in the July-September issue of *Hound and Horn*. Apparently the idea for a poem on Lee had been in his mind for some time and his reading in Southern history and his serious considerations of Southern problems undoubtedly pushed these half-formed concepts to a prominent position in his creative consciousness. When he left Georgia in the late spring for

---

Nashville. Davidson says that in the Guntersville meeting the Agrarians discussed, among other topics, the means by which they could give literary emphasis to the forthcoming journal.

his teaching assignment at Bread Loaf, the idea for the poem was beginning to take shape. In late August he committed to paper a draft of a poem which at that time was called "General Lee Remembers." This first written draft, which contains only sixty-one lines, differs in many essential respects from the final version of 121 lines completed in January, 1934, and read later in the same month in Nashville at a United Daughters of the Confederacy luncheon. Starting with this first draft in August, 1933, and including the final one in January of the next year, Davidson wrote five versions of the poem that is now "Lee in the Mountains." All of them exist in manuscript, and a close reading of them not only shows the evolution of Davidson's best-known poem but also furnishes a concrete example of some of the specific ways a work by one of the Fugitives was affected by the frank criticism of another member of the group. When Davidson had completed the fourth draft of the poem—what he apparently thought was the final version—he sent it to Allen Tate for comment. At Benfolly, Tate's home near Clarksville, Tennessee, Tate and his wife, Caroline Gordon, read the poem; Tate's letter of January 19, three days after he had received the poem, and his comments in the margins of the manuscript indicate the reactions of these two close friends of Davidson's.

Davidson has described the manner in which a typical Fugitive meeting was conducted,[3] and many critics have commented upon the unique nature of the communal efforts of this group. Some have expressed the belief that the renaissance in Southern literature would not have occurred "without the vigorous movement in criticism which preceded it,"[4] and the

3. Donald Davidson, *Southern Writers in the Modern World* (Athens: University of Georgia Press, 1958), pp. 21–22.
4. Richmond Croom Beatty, *et al.*, editors, *The Literature of the South* (Chicago: Scott, Foresman and Co., 1952), p. 613.

work of the Fugitive group has been cited as the outstanding example of the values that accrue when a group of poet-critics discuss in detail each other's poetry.[5] Although the values of this procedure are generally recognized, no one has provided an actual example of the process at work. Davidson's revision of "Lee in the Mountains" in the light of Tate's comments demonstrates how one Fugitive poet was able to incorporate into his work some of the suggestions offered by his fellow poet and critic.

Here is Davidson's description of a typical Fugitive meeting:

First we gave strict attention, from the beginning, to the *form* of poetry. The very nature of our meeting facilitated and intensified such attention, and probably influenced Fugitive habits of composition. Every poem was read aloud by the poet himself, while the members of the group had before them typed copies of the poem. The reading aloud might be followed by a murmur of compliments, but often enough there was a period of ruminative silence before anyone said a word. Then discussion began, and it was likely to be ruthless in its exposure of any technical weakness as to rhyme, meter, imagery, metaphor and was often minute in analysis of details.

.   .   .   .

This process of intensive criticism, characteristic of the Fugitive meetings, carried over into private conversation between meetings when we could discuss our poems more informally. It was still more highly developed in the correspondence and exchange of manuscripts when this or that member was absent from Nashville. I will venture to say that this latter type of criticism was more beneficial, because it allowed deliberation. The most helpful criticism I ever received—and the sternest—was from Allen Tate, in the marginal notations on manuscripts that I sent him and in the very frank letters that always came with the return of a manuscript.[6]

5. Louise Cowan, *The Fugitive Group* (Baton Rouge: Louisiana State University Press, 1959), p. xix.
6. Davidson, *op. cit.*, p. 21.

In the letter to Tate dated January 15, 1934, which was included in the package containing the "Lee in the Mountains" manuscript, Davidson remarks: "I am painfully aware that my conception far outruns my execution in this poem. I am not in the least satisfied with it." The poem at this time had gone through four complete versions and was yet to be considerably revised before it was published for the first time in the May, 1934, issue of the *American Review*, but, as Davidson's remarks imply, his original conception prevailed throughout, and it was only in the strengthening and enlargement of the execution that there was revision. The first draft is only half the finished product and only eight lines of the original effort appear unchanged in the published version. It is obvious, however, that before he first put pen to paper the poet had clearly in mind the poem he would finally write. When Davidson stopped abruptly after sixty-one lines, he had presented, although in different language and a somewhat different tone, the material that appears in the first eighty lines of the completed poem.

The subject matter of the poem, covering the period between 1865 and 1870 while Lee was President of Washington College, may be divided into five parts, all presented through Lee's stream of consciousness. In Part One (ll. 1–17), as he walks across the campus toward his office, Lee is greeted by a group of students who are seated on the steps waiting for the bell to announce the daily chapel and the beginning of another day's activities. In Part Two (ll. 18–52), Lee goes into his office and resumes the labor that consumed most of his free time during these years, a revision of his father's memoirs. In Part Three (ll. 53–80), Lee ponders a question to which he must have given much attention during this crucial period of his life: Instead of attempting to justify his father's actions during and after the Revolutionary War, why is he not concentrating on his own experiences as leader of the military forces of the Confederacy? In Part Four (ll. 81–103), he gives the reasons for his choice and explores his present situation. In Part Five (ll. 104–121), after Lee's reminiscence is interrupted by the bell calling him to chapel, President Lee presents in essence the remarks he must have given almost daily to the students who looked to him for inspiration and leadership.[7]

The first draft of the poem, "General Lee Remembers," presents almost all of the material included in the first three parts of the completed poem.

[Draft One]

GENERAL LEE REMEMBERS

                 into   shadows
Walking ~~under~~ the ~~elms,~~ walking alone   1

                            the   locusts
From the hitching-rack under / shadow of ~~elms~~   2

Up to the President's office. Hearing the voices   3

Whispering, *Hush, it is General Lee.* ~~Boys,~~   4

~~Take off your hats to General Lee.~~

And the soldiers' faces under the gleam of flags   5

7. Lawrence Bowling, "An Analysis of Davidson's 'Lee in the Mountains,'" *Georgia Review*, VI (Spring, 1952), pp. 69–88.

Lifting no more on any road or field   6

is
Where ~~still~~ Virginia still, though lost and gone   7

perished, remembering
Sunken, and lost, and ~~tired, waiting the~~ bugles.   8

Walking the rocky path; and the columns old   9

stones
Where the paint cracks and the grass grows in the plank   10

It is Robert   civilian   who walks.
~~And General~~ Lee in his dark / suit ~~is walking~~   11

~~Under the~~
Lost in ~~In~~ the shadow of elms where no flag flies   12

his
My father's house is taken and ~~the~~ hearth   13

~~Cold as a sword that~~

Left to the candle-drippings, sown with ashes   14

Moveless as are the dreams, no more renewed   15

I cannot remember my father's hand, I cannot   16

~~Speak to~~

It is not General Lee

Answer his voice as he calls from the misty   17

Mounting where riders gather at gates,   18

~~And day break comes too far away.~~

        then
~~And~~ He was old/, I knew him not, His hand   19

Was stretched for
~~Put down to~~ mine, at daybreak snatched away   20

As he rode out and came no more. The grave   21

Lies in a far land and keeps the vow   22

I made there, once, in better days, yet knew   23

The savor of my fortune even then   24

As a man beholds with certain eyes, the drift   25

Of time, and tongues of men, and a sacred cause.   26

The fortune of the Lees is with the land   27

My father's land, which once I left. My mother   28

Knew this well, and sat among the candles   29

Reading the *Memoirs*, now so long unread   30

These faces and these voices and his hand,   31

Gone from the dream—they are Virginia still   32

The pen marches, the pages grow, the South   33

Knew my father and yet again will know   34

Ah, but to tell the tale. What's history   35

Now but a wraith clutched out of the mist,   36

                                    a
Where voices are loud and ~~the~~ glut of little souls   37

In all the too much blood and the perished battles   38

What I will do is only a son's devoir   39

To a lost father, to my mother's husband   40

The rest must stay unsaid and lips be locked   41

If it were said—   42

The rivers now run clear in Virginia's Valley   43

Clear of blood and the weeping of old women   44

Rises no more. The waves of grain begin   45

The Shenandoah is golden with new grain   46

The Blue Ridge, lapped in a haze of light   47

Harbors no war, and is at peace. The columns   48 is

Pass no more; the horse ~~stands~~ at plough; the rifle   49

Returns to the chimney crotch and the hunter's hand   50

This is the peace of bondage, and I wait   51

                      locusts

With words unsaid, thus in the shadow of ~~elms.~~   52

If it were said, and the word should run like fire   53

Like living fire into the roots of grass   54

And the sunken flag should kindle like a flame   55

And the stubborn hearts should waken, and the dream   56

Stir like a crippled phantom under the pines   57

And all the slow earth quicken into shouting   58

Above the feet of gathering men, the sword   59

Unsheathed would rush against the ranks   60

Of blue that shepherd us, that bend us into bondage.   61

    After Davidson had completed these sixty-one lines, he had to put the poem aside to return to Nashville for the opening of the fall quarter at Vanderbilt. His duties there must have consumed most of his time for several weeks, so that he probably was able to do little work on the poem until late October or early November. When he could resume his creative labor, it seems, he reworked carefully the portion already composed before attempting to complete the poem. A close examination of the appropriate sections of the second draft shows how carefully the poet worked through the first draft before attempting to finish his poem. The first important change occurs in the title. After writing "General Lee," with the apparent intention of retaining the previous title "General Lee Remembers," he crosses out both words, and the title becomes "Lee in the Mountains."

Most of the alterations in the lines of Draft One are relatively minor. Twenty lines go into the second draft without change: 1, 3, 7, 13, 14, 16, 21, 29, 30, 33, 36, 37, 41, 45, 46, 47, 50, 53, 54 and 58. Sixteen lines are unchanged except for the substitution of one or two words. For example, "And the soldiers' faces under the gleam of flags" becomes "But the soldiers' faces under the gleam of flags." Several other examples indicate the care with which the poet worked with each of the sixty-one lines of Draft One before allowing it to become a part of the revised version:

(Draft 1) Lifting no more on any road or field   Line 6
(Draft 2) Lift no more on any road or field

(1) Walking the rocky path; and the columns old   9
(2) Walking the rocky path, and the stairs are old

(1) Answer his voice as he calls from the misty   17
(2) Answer his voice as he calls far-off in the misty

(1) He was old then, I knew him not, His hand   19
(2) He was old then—I was a child—his hand

(1) Was stretched for mine, at daybreak snatched away   20
(2) Stretched for mine, some faint dawn snatched away

(1) As he rode out and came no more. The grave   21
(2) And he rode out and came no more. The grave

(1) Lies in a far land and keeps the vow   22
(2) Of Henry Lee in a far land still keeps

(1) I made there, once, in better days, yet knew   23
(2) The vow I made in better days, nor knew

(1) The fortune of the Lees is with the land   27
(2) The fortune of the Lees goes with the land

(1) Knew my father and yet again will know   34
(2) Knew my father once and again will know

(1) Ah, but to tell the tale. What's history   35
(2) Ah, but to tell the tale. What is history

(1) With words unsaid, thus in the shadow of locusts   52
(2) With words unsaid, thus in the shadow of doom

(1) Stir like a crippled phantom under the pines   57
(2) Stir like an avenging phantom under the pines

In six other lines the basic idea expressed in Draft One is given sharper focus by a change of phrasing:

(1) Sunken and lost and perished, remembering bugles   8
(2) Sunken and spent, remembering only the bugles

(1) Lost in the shadow of elms where no flags flies   12
(2) Bound in the shadow of doom where no flag flies

(1) Moveless as are the dreams, no more renewed   15
(2) Sifted and tossed like dreams that now are cold

(1) As a man beholds with certain eyes, the drift   25

Of time, and tongues of men, and a sacred cause
(2)   God too late

Unseals to certain eyes the drift
Of time, and the tongues of men, and a sacred cause.

(1) The Blue Ridge, lapped in a haze of light   47
     Harbors no war, and is at peace. . . .
(2) The Blue Ridge, lapped in a haze of light,
     Thunders no more. . . .

(1) This is the peace of bondage, and I wait   51
     With words unsaid, thus in the shadow of locusts.
(2) To keep this peace of bondage and to wait
     With words unsaid, thus in the shadow of doom.

Draft Two runs to 130 lines and includes all the content of the published version of the poem. In addition, this draft contains twenty-seven lines that appear without change in the published poem. Nine lines longer than the final version, the second draft contains some material that will subsequently be dropped and several extensive revisions that demonstrate the poet's attempts to evoke the desired response from the reader. Near the beginning of both versions, Davidson strives to establish Lee's relationship with the students of Washington College, the devotion and love which these young men must have felt for their revered leader. In Draft One, the poet wrote:

Hearing the voices
Whispering, *Hush, it is General Lee. Boys*
Take off your hats to General Lee.

Obviously dissatisfied with this statement, he deleted the sentence "*Boys / Take off your hats to General Lee*" and moved on without trying to recast it. In his revision, however, he returned to the same point and wrote:

> Hearing the voices
> Whisper, *Hush it is General Lee.* The boys
> Tip their hats to General Lee.

Still not pleased, he crossed out "The boys / Tip their hats to General Lee" and wrote "Young men, / Receive the loneliness of this salute to you." Although he allowed this version to stand temporarily, the passage was considerably revised in subsequent drafts of the poem.

A little later in the poem Davidson is trying to suggest the disparate elements competing for Lee's consciousness—his family associations and his experiences in the Civil War. In the first draft Davidson wrote:

> My mother
> Knew this well, and sat among the candles
> Reading the *Memoirs,* now so long unread
> These faces and these voices and his hand
> Gone from the dream—they are Virginia still
> The pen marches, the pages grow, . . .

In the second draft the poet attempts to present this conflict more concretely by indicating specific elements:

> My mother
> Knew this well and sat among the candles
> Reading the *Memoirs,* now so long unread.
> Her voice, his hand, the flags, the soldiers faces
> A dream's gone desire—these are Virginia still
> The pen marches, the pages grow . . .

This crucial passage will be considerably worked over in each of the later revisions before the poet finds the imagery to blend these two important groups of experiences.

A comparison of two other brief passages points up how Davidson succeeds in communicating Lee's reflections more vividly and concretely. The South is now at peace, and surely one would choose this scene in which "clear waters run in Virginia's Valley," rather than the slaughters of war that fill the rivers with blood and the house with "the weeping of young women."

[DRAFT ONE]

> If it were said—
> The rivers now run clear in Virginia's Valley
> Clear of blood and the weeping of old women
> Rises no more. The waves of grain begin
> The Shenandoah is golden with new grain
> The Blue Ridge, lapped in a haze of light
> Harbors no war, and is at peace . . .

[DRAFT TWO]

> If it were said, as it cannot be said
> I see clear waters run in Virginia's Valley,
> And in the house the weeping of young women
> Rises no more. The waves of grain begin.
> The Shenandoah is golden with new grain
> The Blue Ridge, lapped in a haze of light,
> Thunders no more . . .

The imagery of the revised passage is more effective because it is more restrained (there are no rivers of blood) and yet it is more dramatic: now it is *young*, not *old*, women who are no longer weeping; the rather trite statement "The

Blue Ridge . . . / Harbors no war" becomes more sug-
gestively "The Blue Ridge . . . / Thunders no more."

Davidson concludes his first draft with Lee's considering
what might have happened if he had chosen another course
of action, if he had decided—or if he were yet to decide—to
issue a call to arms. (Such a call might have seemed justifi-
able because of the general belief that the victor had violated
the terms of the agreement at Appomattox.) In its first
form the passage that indicated the reaction of the former
soldiers to an expression of dissatisfaction from Lee was:

> If it were said, and the word should run like fire
> Like living fire into the roots of grass
> And the sunken flag should kindle like a flame
> And the stubborn hearts should waken, and the dream
> Stir like a crippled phantom under the pines
> And all the slow earth quicken into shouting
> Above the feet of gathering men, the sword
> Unsheathed would rush against the ranks
> Of blue that shepherd us, that bend us into bondage.

In Draft Two this passage is considerably revised:

> If it were said and the word should run like fire
> Like living fire into the roots of grass,
> The sunken flag would kindle on the hills
> The stubborn hearts would waken, and the dream
> Stir like an avenging phantom under the pines
> And all the slow earth quicken into shouting
> Beneath the feet of gathering men—the sword
> Locks in the sheath. The sword of Lee
> Bows to the rust that cankers, and the guns
> Mouldering keep the forlorn peace of bondage.

In the revised form the results of Lee's decision to call again upon his former soldiers are positively and decisively stated: "The sunken flag would kindle" and "the stubborn hearts would waken" (note the change from the conditional "should" of Draft One); "the dream / [would] Stir like an avenging phantom" (in the first version it was a "crippled phantom"). But here Lee retreats quickly before the almost certain repercussion of this decision, a reaction much nearer that of Lee in the published poem. In the first draft "the sword / Unsheathed would rush against the ranks / Of blue that shepherd us, that bend us into bondage." But now President Lee in the quietness of his study, almost as quickly as the thought flashes across his consciousness, realizes he cannot entertain the thought of resuming the war. Despite the obvious provocation, what he must do is clear. "The sword of Lee / Bows to the rust that cankers, and the guns / Mouldering keep the forlorn peace of bondage."

With the resolution of this crux, the poet moves on to complete the poem. Now that Lee has made his choice, he continues his anguished examination of his present situation.

> Among these boys, whose eyes lift up to mine
> Within these walls where droning wasps repeat
> A sinister reveille, I still must face
> The grim flag-bearer thundering with his summons
> Once more to surrender, now to surrender all.

Among the most unpleasant of his memories is his recollection that he foresaw the disastrous conclusion of the war before the others did and strongly suspects he could have altered its course.[8]

8. That Lee seriously considered the possibility of taking his army to the mountains and continuing the war from there is indicated by a statement made by Jefferson Davis, President of the Confederate States, at a

The mountains, once I said, in the little room
At Richmond, by the huddled fire, and still
The President shook his head. The mountains wait,
I said, in the long beat and rattle of siege, and the
    thunder
Of cratered Petersburg. Too late, too late,
We sought the mountains, and those people came.

So he is "in the mountains now beyond Appomattox /
Listening long for voices that will not speak / Again." At
this point the poet has difficulty rendering the specific details
that this memory recalls.
First he writes:

. . . waiting the rapid hoofs of the courier a rider
To lift the flap and enter. Is it the plume
Of Stuart? It is the form of Hill? A. P. Hill
The red beard
The rough step of Early.

But this passage is deleted and he writes:

. . . hearing the hoofbeats come and go and fade
Without a stop, without a brown hand lifting
The tent-flap, under the shadow of locusts,
Nor even on the long white road the flag
Of Jackson's quick brigades or the eyes of Hill
Flashing through dust and musketry or Stuart
Laughing beneath his plume.

---

memorial service for General Lee, November 3, 1870, and reported in the
Richmond *Dispatch*, November 4, 1870: "When in the last campaign he
was beleaguered at Petersburg, and painfully aware of the straits to which
we were reduced, he said, 'With my army in the mountains of Virginia
I could carry on this war for twenty years longer.' . . . In surrender he
anticipated conditions that have not been fulfilled." (Quoted by Hudson
Strode in *Jefferson Davis: Tragic Hero: The Last Twenty-five Years,
1864–1889.* New York: Harcourt, Brace & World, 1964, p. 370.)

Even in its revised form most of this passage will be dropped in the next draft of the poem, as will the one that follows.

> I am alone
> Trapped, consenting, taken, at last in the mountains.
> My people, we must wait—it is useless now
> To rise against the Myrmidons. Tall Troy is fallen
> So let us wait and waiting hush the murmur
> Of bitter cries until our time is come.

At this point the mediations are interrupted by the bell calling him to chapel, and Draft Two ends, as the succeeding ones will, with the presentation of Lee's remarks before the students in chapel, an affirmation of faith in a just and merciful God who will never forsake "His children and his children's children forever / To all generations of the faithful heart. Amen."

There is apparently no way to determine exactly the amount of time that elapsed between the completion of the second and third drafts of the poem. Davidson recalls that he devoted a major portion of the time he could allow for creative activity during the fall and early winter of 1933 to the writing and rewriting of this poem. Since he did not complete the first draft until early September, did not begin the second draft until the first or second week in October, and finished two more completely revised versions of the poem before he wrote Tate on January 15, 1934—the diligence with which he pursued his task is most evident.[9]

Draft Three contains 118 lines and includes 22 lines, in addition to the 8 of Draft One and the 30 of Draft Two,

9. Davidson says on this point, "I may have been under pressure from Allen Tate to furnish a poem for the forthcoming 'poetry number' of the *American Review.* I can't remember all this with absolute clearness, but am sure a poem was wanted from me." Note Tate's reference to "our A.R. exhibit," p. 41.

that appear unchanged in the first published version of the poem. After two thorough rewritings of his first attempt, then, the poet has written 60 lines—almost half the completed poem—with which he will remain satisfied through the two remaining revisions.

Again, a detailed comparison of Draft Two and Draft Three is enlightening in tracing the development of the poem. Draft Two is important because in it the poet first got down on paper the essential content of his poem, and Draft Three reveals the painstaking efforts of the artist as he attempts to mould his material into its final form. Davidson's revisions of Draft Two are not predominantly concerned with word changes and changes within lines. These are yet to come. (Fifty-seven lines are carried forward without change. In twenty-one others there is the substituting of but one or two words.) The alterations that do occur, however, are significant. In some instances, the poet is apparently attempting to make the poetic experience more vivid and accessible. Examples of this sort are many. "Bound in the shadow of doom where no flag flies" becomes "Commanding in a dream where no flag flies." "Left to the candle-drippings, sown with ashes / Sifted and tossed like dreams that now are cold" is changed to "Left to the candle-drippings where the ashes / Whirl as the chimney breathes on the cold stone."

Some of the changes are apparently an effort to enhance the sensuous quality of the verse. In line 30, for example, "Reading the *Memoirs*" becomes "Fingering the *Memoirs*." The passage beginning at line 36 has been altered for a similar purpose. In Draft Two, it reads:

Ah, but to tell the tale. What is history
Now but a wraith and a clutching out of the mist

Where voices are loud and a glut of little souls
Laps at the too much blood and the perished battles.

In Draft Three, this passage is significantly altered by the insertion of a simple question, the rearrangement of the word order, and the substitution of a few words.

Why did my father write? Did he foresee
History clutched as a wraith in blowing mist
Where voices are loud, and a glut of little souls
Laps at the too much blood and the perished battles.

Perhaps the best example of the revision of the loose, abstractly phrased exclamation to the sharp imagistic presentation found in good poetry may be seen in the two versions of the passage beginning at line 41:

They will have their say, and I shall not have mine
But with my father's pen that wrote in vain
Of old neglected forays and lost triumphs
I write, in vain, and tell what can be told
The rest must go unsaid, and the lips be locked.

In Draft Three it is expanded to read:

He had his say, then—I shall not have mine
What I must do is only a son's devoir
To a long-lost father—let him speak for me
The rest must pass to men who never knew
The grim and sure out-reach of moving armies
Or heard the keen Confederate battle-cry
Behind the spinning smoke or saw the tense
Eyes of Virginia boys encounter death.
I write—in vain—I tell what can be told
The rest must go unsaid and the lips be locked.

As one would suspect, not all attempts of this kind were so successful as this one—and even this passage will be further refined in Draft Four. The five-line passage beginning at line 55 of Draft Two, though considerably altered in Draft Three, does not appear in Draft Four. The Draft Two version goes as follows:

> There is no war, and yet there is no peace.
> I gave my word and was betrayed
> And did I thus betray? And did I vow
> To keep the peace of bondage and to wait
> With words unsaid, thus in the shadow of doom.

In Draft Three it reads:

> But still the raven tears my heart? Is this
> The peace to which I bowed my head. It is
> A peace of bondage grinding me to wait
> With words unsaid, here in the shadow of doom.

It is revealing also to note the parts of Draft Two that are omitted from Draft Three. There are three rather conspicuous omissions: lines 75–79, 92–97, and 108–111.

> This is the last Gethsemane of men who love
> A land and people close as a mother's breast
> I had rather die a thousand deaths, but cannot
> Die as a soldier dies. In the crumpled paper,
> The scratching paper and the blotter of memory

> But Lee is in the mountains now, in Virginia mountains
> And all that I thought or dreamed of once is done
> If I had known what now I know, when day
> Breaks with a silent message and no thunder
> Of guns, no bugle call, no tramp of men
> I would not go to this surrender armless, so,

My people, we must wait—it is useless now
To rise against the Myrmidons. Tall Troy is fallen
So let us wait and waiting hush the murmur
Of bitter cries until our time is come

The deletion of these lines is not the result of the poet's changing his mind about what he wants to say. On the contrary, they state an important aspect of the theme, but too boldly, too directly. In subsequent revisions the poet will express by indirection, will suggest, the sentiment and feeling borne in these lines. Lee's belief that he has been betrayed, that his former enemy has not fulfilled the just and humane terms of surrender, is an important part of the poem. So, too, are Lee's fears that he might have failed to justify the trust placed in him by his followers. In the years between 1865 and 1870, the poet is saying, Lee must have realized that the terms offered at Appomattox were unrealistic. He has been misled by his own sense of honesty and justice. Should he have withdrawn to the mountains and made the enemy seek him out? Small bands of guerrilla warriors could have prolonged the war almost endlessly; perhaps the enemy could have been plagued and molested until his desire for peace was genuine. Understanding of Lee's doubts and questions is preliminary to an understanding of his attitude during the period covered in the poem. But the poet realizes that his mode of expression is wrong. The conflict is so boldly stated that the credible personality of Lee is in danger of being destroyed. The poet is too much involved personally, and this involvement encroaches upon the point of view he has adopted for the poem. The illusion of reality is stronger without these lines than with them; the poetic experience is not disrupted. The reader must share Lee's agonized struggles and not consider with Davidson his opinion of what the situation probably was. The less direct, more suggestive manner in which this basic conflict is presented in the published version of the poem accomplishes this objective completely.

After making the extensive revisions that went into Draft Three, Davidson was well enough satisfied with the poem to prepare a typewritten manuscript to send to Allen Tate for his comments. The search to find the exact manner of expressing the poet's conception of Lee's character continues, apparently, even during the actual typewriting. Although sixty-three lines of Draft Three go unchanged into Draft Four, the never-ending process of refinement goes on. There are numerous examples of the poet's attempt to make his references more specific and meaningful: "my hearth" becomes "his hearth" (14); "And all the torn earth" is changed to "And this torn earth" (73); "the land" to "this land" (27); and "On these green altars" to "On your altars" (105). There are examples, too, of the poet's substituting an evocative connotative word for one less suggestive: "stubborn hearts" becomes "brooding hearts" (71); "avenging phantom," "crippled phantom" (72);[10] "gathering men," "ragged men" (74). Davidson's acute sensitivity to the musical quality of the line, a dominant trait in all of his best poetry, is undoubtedly responsible for the shift of word order in lines 111 and 112. The lines that appear in Draft Three as "And the fierce undying faith / And the quenchless love" are simply and effectively rearranged to read "And the fierce faith undying / And the love quenchless."

Many of the emendations are the result of the poet's efforts to substitute an image for the simple statement or

10. He had written "crippled phantom" in the first draft.

to sharpen, to make more concrete and specific, the existing image. Thus, "Where the sun breaks through a ruined shadow of locusts" becomes "Where the sun falls through the ruined boughs of locusts" (2); "For the soldiers' faces under the gleam of flags" is changed to "But the soldiers' faces under the tossing flags" (5); "Where paint cracks and grass grows in the stone" is changed to "And paint cracks and grass eats on the stone" (9); "An outlaw in his own land, a voice / Commanding in a dream where no flag flies" becomes "An outlaw fumbling for the latch, a voice / Commanding in a dream where no flag flies" (12–13). This last emendation is particularly important because the poet has found an image that suggests Lee's predicament and sets the tone for his opening section. Lee is in fact an outlaw; and, at this point, he is actually "fumbling for the latch" that will open the door to his office; so the lines take the reader with Lee as he crosses the campus and reaches his office door (after he opens the door and enters the office, the second section of the poem begins—his meditations as he resumes work on his father's memoirs). But the phrase suggests, more significantly, the fundamental conflict of the poem: How is Lee, a man without official power or position, to assist the thousands of people—the students at Washington College and the residents of the South generally—who are looking to him for leadership in these "Black Raven Days of Reconstruction"? What course of action can he or should he take?

An examination of the alterations of the passage beginning at line 81 reveals the poet's endeavoring to rid his poem of excess verbiage and to make his projection of Lee's dilemma more graphic. In Draft Three, this passage is:

I face what once I saw, before others knew,
A phantom rising where the flags reeled down
Within the smoke of Gettysburg or the tangled
Cry of the Wilderness wounded, bloody with doom,
The cold and last solution of all striving.

The revised form is more effective:

Without arms or men I stand, but with bitter
    knowledge
I face what long I saw, before others knew
When Pickett's men streamed back and I heard the
    tangled
Cry of the Wilderness wounded, bloody with doom.

On January 15, 1934, when Davidson had completed Draft
Four, the first typewritten manuscript of his poem, he sent
a copy to Allen Tate, and it was this copy that Tate and
Caroline Gordon read at Benfolly. In his accompanying letter, Davidson called his poem "a tentative draft"—despite
the fact that it had undergone many revisions and had been
completely rewritten three times—and indicated his dissatisfaction with its present state. "I am not in the least satisfied with it," he wrote; "I don't know whether it will ever
do. But I want you to see the poem."

Apparently Tate read the poem immediately, for he returned it on January 19, 1934, and, along with the marginal
comments, he sent a rather long letter:

Your Lee poem is the finest you have ever written. I say this
deliberately after much meditation and study of it. I thought your other
recent poems, in the last couple of years, too argumentative and
documentary. This new one is about Lee and about a great deal
more than Lee. It is a very fine poem. If you lose what you've
got here and relapse into documentation, I shall come over and cut
your ears off!

[Draft Four]

LEE IN THE MOUNTAINS
1865–1870

Walking into the shadows, walking alone   1

Where the sun falls through the ruined boughs of locusts,   2

Up to the president's office.[a] Hearing the voices   3

Whisper, *Hush it is General Lee!*   4

But the soldiers' faces under the tossing flags   5

Lift no more by any road or field,   6

And I am spent with battle and old[b] sorrow.   7

Walking the rocky path, where the steps decay   8

And the paint cracks and grass eats on the stone.   9

It is not General Lee, young men . . .   10

It is Robert Lee in a dark civilian suit who walks,   11

An outlaw fumbling for the latch, a voice   12

a. Tate indicates that a paragraph division should come here and points out "a little abrupt as it is punctuated." His other comments, written in the margins of Draft Four, will be given in footnotes; the places at which they occur in the text will be indicated by superscript letters.
b. "More definite?"

Commanding in a dream where no flag flies.[c]   13

My father's house is taken and his hearth   14

Left to the candle-drippings where the ashes   15

Whirl at a chimney-breath on the cold stone.   16

I can hardly remember my father's look, I cannot   17

Answer his voice as he calls farewell in the misty   18

Mounting where riders gather at gates.   19

He was old then—I was a child—his hand   20

Held out for mine, some daybreak snatched away,   21

And he rode out, a beaten man. Now let   22

surer

His lone grave keep, ~~deeper~~ than cypress roots   23

The vow I made beside him. God too late   24

Unseals to certain eyes the drift   25

Of time and the hopes of men and a sacred cause.   26

c. "See letter" [Tate is referring to his letter to Davidson, previously cited. See p. 28.]

The fortune of the Lees goes with this land   27

Whose sons can keep it still. My mother   28

Told me much. She sat among the candles,   29

Fingering the *Memoirs*, now so long unread,   30

And as my pen moves on across the page   31

Her voice comes back, a filmy[d] distillation   32

Of old Virginia splendors[e] done to death,   33

The hurt of all that was and cannot be.   34

Why did my father write? I know he saw   35

History clutched as a wraith out of blowing mist   36

Where voices are loud, and a glut of little souls   37

Laps at the too much blood and the burning house.   38

He would have his say, but I shall not have mine.   39

What I do is only a son's devoir   40

To a lost father. Let him only speak.   41

d. "omit adjective?"
e. "Is this word in character?"

The rest must pass to men who never knew   42

(But on a written page) the strike of armies,   43

And never heard the long Confederate war-cry[f]   44

Charge through the muzzling smoke or saw the bright   45

Eyes of the beardless boys go up to death.[g]   46

It is Robert Lee who writes with his father's hand—   47

The rest must go unsaid and the lips be locked.   48

If all were told, as it cannot be told—   49

If all the dread opinion of the heart   50

Now could speak, now in the shame and torment   51

Lashing the bound and trampled States—   52

If a word were said, as it cannot be said—   53

I see clear waters run in Virginia's Valleys,   54

f. Tate encircles "war" and notes "Read line without this. Isn't it better?"
g. Tate places parentheses around lines 45 and 46 and exclaims "Fine!"

And in the house the weeping of young women   55

Rises no more. The waves of grain begin.   56

The Shenandoah is golden with new grain.   57

The Blue Ridge, lapped in a haze of light,   58

Thunders no more. The horse is at plough. The rifle   59

Returns to the chimney crotch and the hunter's hand.   60

And nothing else than this? Was it for this   61

                        our
That on an April day we stacked ~~the~~ arms   62

Obedient to a soldier's trust—to sink, to lie   63

Ground by the vaunting heels of little men,   64

Forever maimed, defeated, lost, impugned?   65

And was I then betrayed? Did I betray?   66

If it were said, as still it might be said—   67

If it were said, and a word should run like fire,   68

Like living fire into the roots of grass,   69

The sunken flag would kindle on wild hills,   70

The brooding hearts would waken, and the dream   71

Stir like a crippled phantom under the pines,   72

And this torn earth would quicken into shouting   73

Beneath the feet of ragged men—   74
                              The sword

Locks in its sheath, the sword of Robert Lee   75

Bows to the rust that cankers and the silence.[h]   76

Among these boys whose eyes lift up to mine   77

Within gray walls where droning wasps repeat   78

A fumbling reveille, I still must face   79

Day after day, the courier with his summons   80

Once more to surrender, now to surrender all.   81

Without arms or men I stand, but with bitter knowldege[i] 82

h. Tate places parentheses around lines 75 and 76 and comments, "*Sword* too conventional. Not dramatic, but oratorical and I think out of Lee's psychology. Preceding lines so good they deserve better than this."
i. Tate encircles "bitter" and places a question mark above it. After "knowledge" he writes in "only." Apparently he is recommending that this line read, "Without arms or men I stand, but with knowledge only."

I face what long I saw, before others knew   83

When Pickett's men streamed back and I heard the
    tangled   84

Cry of the Wilderness wounded, bloody with doom.   85

The mountains, once I said, in the little room   86

At Richmond, by the huddled fire, but still   87

The President shook his head. The mountains wait,   88

I said in the long beat and rattle of siege   89

At cratered Petersburg. Too late   90

We sought the mountains and those people came.   91

And Lee is in mountains now, beyond Appomattox,   92

Listening long for voices that never will speak   93

Again; hearing the hoofbeats come and go and fade   94

Without a stop, without a brown hand lifting   95

The tent-flap, or a bugle call at dawn,   96

Or ever on the long white road the flag   97

Of Jackson's quick brigades. I am alone,   98

Trapped, consenting, taken at last in mountains.   99

It is not the bugle now, or the long roll beating.[j]   100

The simple stroke of a chapel bell forbids   101

The hurtling dream, recalls the lonely wound.[k]   102

Young men, the God of your fathers is a just   103

And merciful God who in this blood once shed   104

On your green altars measures out all days,   105

And measures out the grace   106

Whereby alone we live;   107

And in His might He waits,   108

Brooding within the certitude of time,   109

To bring this lost forsaken valor   110

And the fierce faith undying   111

And the love quenchless   112

j. "From here on it is magnificent."
k. "Does this mean Jackson? Or his own sorrow? If that why not *mind?*"

To flower among the hills to which we cleave,   113

To fruit upon the mountains whither we flee,   114

Never forsaking, never denying   115

His children and His children's children forever   116

Unto all generations of the faithful heart. Amen.   117

Donald Davidson

Despite Tate's general approval of the poem, he wrote that he "must carp a little over details" because he thought in certain particulars the poem could be improved. In addition to the specific suggestions written on the manuscript itself, in his letter Tate commented in more detail on the opening passage.

> It seems to me that the opening lines are far too pat and abrupt. A more halting introduction to the theme, as if from the scattered images of a moment a line of meditation suddenly took hold and went through to its end, is what you want. At present the opening is oratorical, almost set; but you want to make it dramatic.

Then in the forthright manner that was characteristic of the Fugitives' recommendations for improving a fellow poet's work, Tate proposes a major change in the opening of the poem. He points out, however, that he is not presenting a suggestion for Davidson to adopt literally. His rewriting of the opening lines merely attempts to demonstrate "what the dramatic effect might be":

Walking in the shadows, walking alone . . .
The sun falls through the ruined boughs of locusts
Walk to the president's office . . .
                        The president!
A boy mumbles *Hush it is General Lee!*
The soldiers' faces under the tossing flags, etc., etc.,

As Tate had indicated earlier in the letter, his objections
to the opening of the poem were that it was "too pat and
abrupt." He is suggesting a "more halting introduction to the
theme," and he proceeds to discuss his suggestion in more
detail.

And at the end of the passage why not interpolate a line or two or
three of perfectly inconsequential observation on Lee's part. Make him
see for a second a pile of rocks by the path, or a bush, on the fringe
of his gathering meditation; even make the statement of this bold and
flat. You have no idea what dramatic effect, what context it would
give the whole poem. Powerful as the conclusion is, it would be twice
again as powerful. You have let Lee speak but you have not let us
see him. Just make him say: I must have those rocks moved; or that
spirea will bloom in two weeks, it should have been trimmed; or
anything like that.

That Tate had shown the poem to Caroline Gordon and
discussed the proposed change with her is revealed by the
paragraph he added as a postscript to the letter.

Caroline thinks the dramatic effect might be achieved by having him
address the casual remarks to some boys standing by. . . . I might add that
while such an interpolation would be outside your "form," it would
really by its slight violence establish the form. The interpolated passage
might even be put into parenthesis.

Davidson's reaction to Tate's suggestions is revealed most
dramatically in the revisions which he made after he received
Tate's letter and marginal comments. Obviously following
Tate's suggestion, Davidson attempted to provide a "more
halting introduction to the theme" by giving a paragraph

break at the end of line three and by adding a three-line
passage that begins in the middle of line five:

> *Good morning, boys.*
> *(Don't get up. You are early. It is long*
> *Before the bell. You will have long to wait*
> *On these cold steps. . . .)*

Tate had pointed out that the opening of the poem should
be more dramatic and that Davidson could make it more
dramatic by letting Lee speak without violating the unity of
form (the poem is an interior monologue). Tate gives
Caroline Gordon's suggestion that the remarks be addressed
to some boys standing by and adds that "the interpolated passage might even be put into parenthesis." Up to this point,
it is clear that the poet followed these suggestions to the
letter.

One can see, however, that Davidson did not accept completely Tate's recommendations, although it is obvious that
Tate's comments stimulated the creative activity that greatly
strengthened the first section of the poem. Tate suggested that
Lee's remarks be "casual" and "inconsequential," that his
observations—though "directed to the students"—be unre-
lated to the primary matters of the poem. But Lee's remarks,
as Davidson presents them, are undeniably related to the rest
of the poem; in fact, at the outset they suggest clearly and
forcefully its essential conflict. As Lee walks toward his
office he is observed by the students who are awaiting the bell
that will summon them to the morning assembly. When he
approaches the steps where they sit, one student respectfully
hushes the noise of their conversation and all of them rise
and speak to General Lee. The man formerly a general and
now a college president speaks, tells his students not to rise,

and makes the casual and polite comments that one would expect from him: "You are early. It is long / Before the bell. You will have long to wait / On these cold steps. . . ." The reason for Lee's speaking has been explained and the persons to whom he speaks have been identified; consequently the reader is not surprised that his visit inside Lee's mind has been interrupted.

Furthermore, the reader is soon aware that Lee's apparently casual remarks are significant. Not only will the students have long to wait before the bell announces the opening of the daily devotions, but also they must await the coming of a new era to the South. Although Lee realizes, as Davidson indicates in the next line of the poem, that "the young have time to wait," it is clear that Lee, "spent with old wars and new sorrow," has not. What he can do, he must do now. In this interpolated passage, then, the poet is able to present Lee's predicament with force and clarity. The reader shares the dilemma Lee faces in his struggles with the problem that confronts him: stripped of all authority, an outlaw in his own land, how can he continue to act honorably and at the same time strengthen in the young the courage to persevere—to maintain their integrity and self-respect and their belief in the enduring virtues of the society that produced them, and to retain their courage when all they value seems "maimed, defeated, lost, impugned"? This conflict, dramatically suggested in Lee's brief comments to the students seated on the cold steps, is resolved in the concluding section of the poem.

Davidson also considers seriously Tate's other suggestions. In line 7, Tate had underlined "old" and asked in the margin "more definite?" The poet changes the line that appeared in Draft Four as "And I am spent with battle and old sorrow"

to "And I am spent with old wars and new sorrow." In line
32 ("Her voice comes back a filmy distillation"), "filmy"
was encircled with the comment "omit adjective?"; Davidson
substitutes for it "murmuring." "Splendors" was underlined
in line 33 ("Of old Virginia splendors done to death") and
"Is this word in character?" was asked. Davidson alters the
line to "Of old Virginia times now faint and gone." In line
44 ("And never heard the long Confederate war-cry") Tate
had suggested the deletion of "war," and the suggestion is
followed. Tate's comments on lines 75 and 76 indicated
genuine concern: "Sword too conventional. Not dramatic,
but oratorical and I think out of Lee's psychology. Preceding
lines so good they deserve better than this." In Draft Four
these lines are:

> The sword
> Locks in its sheath, the sword of Robert Lee
> Bows to the rust that cankers and the silence.

Davidson changes them to:

> The pen
> Turns to the waiting page, the sword
> Bows to the rust that cankers and the silence.

Tate also objected to "wound" in line 101 ("the hurtling
dream, recalls the lonely wound"), and, as Tate had suggested, Davidson substitutes "mind."

In attempting to emphasize that his appreciation of his
friend's poetic achievement is objective, Tate wrote:

> At first I thought (not wishing to give you the benefit of any doubt
> whatever) that I might be moved too much by the subject as such. But
> that was not the case. It will be the chief ornament of our A.R. exhibit.

Tate's reference is to the *American Review* for which he
was at that time preparing a Poetry Supplement. "Lee in the

Mountains" was included in that supplement—along with poems by Randall Jarrell, Howard Baker, Robert Penn Warren, John Gould Fletcher, Janet Lewis, John Peale Bishop, Mark Van Doren, Louis Macneice, Manson Radford, and John Crowe Ransom—and was first published in the *American Review* for May, 1934. There are five variants between that version and the one included in *Lee in the Mountains and Other Poems* (Boston: Houghton Mifflin Company, 1938). Although none of the changes is major, they do indicate the poet's continuing concern, even after the poem had appeared in print, that his conception not "outrun [his] execution in this poem."

(*American Review*)	The tossing flags	9
(Houghton Mifflin)	Their tossing flags	
(AR)	Where the steps decay	12
(HM)	Where steps decay	
(AR)	Lapped in a haze of light.	62
(HM)	Crowned with a haze of light	
(AR)	Obedient to a soldier's trust—to sink, to lie	67
(HM)	Obedient to a soldier's trust? to lie	
(AR)	Unto all generations of the faithful heart. Amen.	121
(HM)	Unto all generations of the faithful heart.	

Everyone is well aware of the dangers involved in trying to describe the creative process. There are, perhaps, as many different procedures as there are poets, or maybe the process varies with each poem, each work of art dictating its own mode of creation. Generally speaking, however, in the creation of "Lee in the Mountains," Davidson seems to have followed an orderly and logical procedure, one that can be detected in the four extant drafts of the poem written before it appeared in print. In creating his best-known poem, Davidson apparently proceeded in a manner somewhat as follows. For many years a supporter of the principles exemplified by Lee as citizen, soldier, and leader, Davidson was thoroughly acquainted with the facts—and with the many interpretations of these facts—that relate to Lee's illustrious career. It appears evident, furthermore, that he had a firm conception of the materials he would use in the entire poem before he began the actual process of composition, because the contents of the sixty-one lines of Draft One remain essentially unchanged in all the subsequent revisions. However, when he was forced to put the poem aside for a few weeks in order to return to Vanderbilt for the opening of the fall quarter, he carefully reworked the language of the completed segment—line by line—before attempting to finish the poem. Then he added the sixty-nine lines that completed Draft Two and, in this draft, included essentially all the subject matter that appears in the published version of the poem. Draft Three constitutes the most thorough of the revisions of form and style. Although new brief passages are added and a few existing ones are dropped, the poet's primary concern is obviously with matters of expression—searching for the exact word or phrase, sharpening the imagery, or increasing textural richness. Although Draft Four contains some interesting and significant emendations, they are not as significant as those in the earlier revisions because they were made, for the most part, during the actual process of typewriting a manuscript for Allen Tate's perusal and for presentation to the meeting of the United Daughters of the Confederacy.

The number and kind of the revisions made after Davidson received Tate's letter and comments reveal the seriousness with which the poet regarded the suggestions of his friend and critic. An examination of the extant drafts of "Lee in the Mountains" and of the Tate comments demonstrates concretely the manner in which the criticism of the Fugitive Group assisted its member poets in their creative efforts; this examination may also give some insight into the mysterious process of creativity itself.

DONALD DAVIDSON

A Bibliography

Explanatory Note

This bibliography is divided into eight Sections:

I. Books, arranged chronologically according to the original date of publication.

II. Pamphlets, arranged chronologically according to the date of publication.

III. Poems, arranged alphabetically according to title.

IV. Essays and articles, arranged alphabetically according to title.

V. Periodical book reviews, arranged alphabetically according to the name of the author of the book reviewed.

VI. Nashville *Tennessean* book-page reviews (1924–1930), arranged alphabetically according to the name of the author of the book reviewed.

VII. Miscellanea, arranged alphabetically according to title.

VIII. Biographical and critical material, arranged alphabetically according to the name of the author, with descriptive annotation.

Individual listings in Section One are subdivided into two units: contents of the book (when composed of poems or essays), and reviews in periodicals and journals. Signed reviews are listed first, alphabetically by reviewer's surname; unsigned reviews and those signed only with initials (except in instances where the reviewer's identity was easily discernible) are listed alphabetically by the name of the publication in which the review appeared. The listings of poems and essays contain information on their initial appearances followed by a chronological list of subsequent reprintings in Davidson's own collections and other publications and anthologies. Some repetition is involved in this procedure, since titles of poems and essays appear in two places, but it is assumed that the user of this bibliography might desire not only a complete list of the places an item has appeared but also an indication of its placement within the structure of a volume of collected writings.

Since some of Davidson's periodical book reviews were reprinted in his books as titled essays, the titles are listed in Section Four with a reference to the appropriate reviews in Section Five. However, to locate the original source of reviews listed under John Tyree Fain's *Spyglass* anthology, the reader should run directly to the appropriate author listing in Section Six, since that volume is composed entirely of selected *Tennessean* reviews (except for the concluding essay "Criticism Outside New York"). Cross references are provided in Section Six for those reviews reprinted in the book.

It should be noted that Section Six is not an index to all Davidson's columns written during his years as editor of the *Tennessean* book page. Only full-scale reviews, signed or initialed by Davidson, are included. Essays on general subjects, advance news on coming books, and literary gossip sometimes composed his weekly review column. Fain provides a sampling of these in his edition of *The Spyglass*. Also, no attempt has been made to identify any of his brief unsigned reviews, since these are of ephemeral value. The importance of this section lies in the opportunity it provides to witness the reactions of a first-rate Southern critic, with well-defined standards, towards the literature of a crucial period in America's literary history.

Section Eight, comprising essays, books, and theses of a critical or biographical nature, is limited to material evaluative of Davidson's life, career, and thought. Most of the material discussing the Fugitive or Agrarian movements in a general way, casually mentioning Davidson or quoting from him, has been left out.

The bibliography is complete through 1964. This limit has been extended in two instances. Reference is made in Section Three to those poems reprinted in William Pratt's new anthology of *The Fugitive Poets,* published in 1965 by E. P. Dutton and Company. Section Eight includes another 1965 item, John Lincoln Stewart's study of the Fugitives and Agrarians, *The Burden of Time,* published by Princeton University Press. Neither Pratt's anthology nor Stewart's study was officially published or available when the bibliography was completed.

Every reasonable effort has been made to make this listing as complete and accurate as possible, although a margin for error and omission in an effort of this kind must be allowed. Every single item has either been viewed firsthand or examined by a trustworthy source. Much of the material was discovered by means of a meticulous examination of Davidson's personal clippings, records, and files. Besides permitting this examination, he graciously agreed to add to the authority of this list by reading it over in manuscript and making additions, corrections, and suggestions—certainly an onerous and intimidating task for a still active literary artist.

It should also be recorded here that Miss Clara Mae Brown of the Joint University Libraries, Nashville, was a never-failing source of effective assistance in locating and verifying numerous items.

The earliest item listed is an undergraduate essay entitled "The Lady or the Tiger," contributed to the January, 1910, issue of the *Vanderbilt Observer*, a campus literary magazine, and the latest is an essay, "Decorum in the Novel," which appeared in the Winter, 1964-65, issue of *Modern Age*. In all, the bibliography includes the titles of 14 books (exclusive of revisions or new editions), 6 pamphlets, 124 poems, and 102 essays and articles. A survey of the book-review sections indicates a total of 65 books reviewed for periodicals and journals and 367 books reviewed for the Nashville *Tennessean* book page. The Miscellanea section contains references to such activities as his periodic editorship of the *Fugitive* magazine and the production of the libretto for an opera, *Singin' Billy*. The quantity of Davidson's literary output is matched by its variety and its quality, and it is hoped that this bibliography will provide the basis for just and accurate assessments of his significance in twentieth-century American literature.

March 1, 1965

I. *Books*

An Outland Piper. (Poems.) Boston and New York: Houghton Mifflin Company, 1924.

Contents

"An Outland Piper," pp. 3–5 · "Old Harp," pp. 6–7 · "The House of the Sun," pp. 8–9 · "The Amulet," pp. 10–11 · "Variation on an Old Theme," pp. 12–14 · "Postscript of a Poor Scholar," p. 15 · "Serenade," pp. 16–18 · "John Darrow," pp. 19–21 · "The Tiger-Woman," pp. 22–23 · "Following the Tiger," pp. 24–26 · "Drums and Brass," pp. 29–30 · "A Dead Romanticist," p. 31 · "Corymba," pp. 32–34 · "Dryad," pp. 35–36 · "Twilight Excursion," pp. 37–38 · "Naiad," pp. 39–40 · "Avalon," pp. 41–43 · "Prie-Dieu," pp. 44–45 · "Redivivus," p. 46 · "Requiescat," pp. 47–48 · "Voice of the Dust," pp. 49–50 · "The Wolf," p. 51 · "Afternoon Call," pp. 52–53 · "The Road to Mort-Homme," p. 54 · "Utterance," p. 55 · "Alla Stoccata," pp. 59–63 · "Ecclesiasticus I," pp. 64–65 · "Ecclesiasticus II," pp. 66–67 · "Iconoclast," pp. 68–69 · "Competition," pp. 70–71 · "Censored," p. 72 · "Pot Macabre," pp. 73–74 · "The Man Who Would Not Die," pp. 77–82.

Signed Reviews

BENÉT, WILLIAM ROSE. New York *Evening Post Literary Review,* July 26, 1924, p. 918.

CLARKE, GEORGE HERBERT. *Sewanee Review,* XXXIII (January, 1924), 105–111.

DABBS, JAMES McBRIDE. Columbia (S.C.) *State,* May 4, 1924.

GREER, HILTON R. Dallas *Morning News,* December 21, 1924.
GUITERMAN, ARTHUR. *Outlook,* CXXXVI (April 16, 1924), 649–650.
McCLURE, JOHN. *Double Dealer,* VI (August–September, 1924), 209–210.
MORTON, DAVID. *Bookman,* LIX (May, 1924), 346–348.
UNTERMEYER, LOUIS. *Yale Review,* XIV (October, 1924), 156–161.

Unsigned Reviews

Boston *Transcript,* May 10, 1924.
Columbia (S.C.) *Record,* March 16, 1924.
Nashville *Banner* (W.A.D.), March 16, 1924.
Nation, CXVIII (April 2, 1924), 376.
New York *Times Book Review,* March 30, 1924, p. 7.
Poetry, XXIV (September, 1924), 344.

The Tall Men. (Poems.) Boston and New York: Houghton Mifflin Company, 1927.

Contents

"Prologue: The Long Street," pp. 1–3 · "The Tall Men," pp. 4–17 · "The Sod of Battle-Fields," pp. 18–27 · "Geography of the Brain," pp. 28–43 · "The Faring," pp. 44–67 · "Conversation in a Bedroom," pp. 68–85 · "The Breaking Mould," pp. 86–95 · "Epithalamion," pp. 96–105 · "Resurrection," pp. 106–112 · "Epilogue: Fire on Belmont Street," pp. 113–117.

Signed Reviews

BENÉT, STEPHEN VINCENT. *Saturday Review of Literature,* IV (December 10, 1927), 425.
EISENBERG, EMANUEL. *Bookman,* LXVI (November, 1927), 328–329.
FLETCHER, JOHN GOULD. *Nation,* CXXVI (January 18, 1928), 71.
HARTSOCK, ERNEST. *Bozart,* I (November–December, 1927), 16.
HUTCHINSON, PERCY. New York *Times Book Review,* November 13, 1927, p. 9.

JENKINS, OLIVER. *Voices,* May, 1928, pp. 322–325.
KNICKERBOCKER, WILLIAM S. *Sewanee Review,* XXXVI (April 1928), 211–224.
McCORMICK, R. E. Knoxville *News-Sentinel,* October 9, 1927.
MONROE, HARRIET. *Poetry,* XXI (January, 1928), 222–224.
POSEY, WILLIS. Asheville *Times,* November 13, 1927.
RANSOM, JOHN CROWE. Nashville *Tennessean,* October 2, 1927.
WINTON, G. B. *Christian Advocate,* LXXXVIII (November 11, 1927), 1420.

Unsigned Reviews
Columbia (S.C.) *State* (J.V.N.), September 25, 1927.
Louisville (Ky.) *Journal Courier,* November 20, 1927.
Nashville *Banner,* September 25, 1927.
New Republic (M.C.), LIII (February 15, 1928), 355.
Raleigh *Times* (M.G.A.), October 1, 1927.

British Poetry of the Eighteen-Nineties. (Anthology.) Garden City, New York: Doubleday, Doran & Company, 1937.

Contains a general Introduction (pp. xix–lii), a bibliography (pp. liii–lxxii), and critical introductions to selections from the poetry of the following authors:

Oscar Wilde, pp. 3–28 · William Ernest Henley, pp. 29–55 · Robert Louis Stevenson, pp. 56–67 · Rudyard Kipling, pp. 68–86 · Aubrey Beardsley, pp. 87–92 · Ernest Dowson, pp. 93–106 · Arthur Symons, pp. 107–127 · Lionel Johnson, pp. 128–153 · John Davidson, pp. 154–180 · Richard Le Gallienne, pp. 181–189 · Laurence Binyon, pp. 190–195 · Eugene Lee-Hamilton, pp. 196–201 · A. E. Housman, pp. 202–217 · Thomas Hardy, pp. 218–232 · Robert Bridges, pp. 233–243 · William Butler Yeats, pp. 244–273 · George William Russell ("AE"), pp. 274–284 · Nora Hopper, pp. 285–294 · Katharine Tynan, pp. 295–310 · Dora Sigerson, pp. 311–324 · "Moira O'Neill," pp. 325–328 · William Sharp ("Fiona Mcleod"), pp. 329–348 · Laurence Housman, pp. 349–357 · Alice Meynell, pp. 358–367 · "Michael Field," pp. 368–377 · Francis Thompson, pp. 378–399 · Gerard Manley Hopkins, pp. 400–408.

Reviews

Atlanta *Constitution,* June 27, 1937.
Chattanooga *News* (A.D.M.), April 23, 1937.
New York *Herald Tribune,* May 16, 1937.

The Attack on Leviathan. Regionalism and Nationalism in the United States. (Essays.) Chapel Hill: The University of North Carolina Press, 1938.

Contents

"The Diversity of America," pp. 3–12 · "Two Interpretations of American History," pp. 13–38 · "Social Science Discovers Regionalism," pp. 39–64 · "Regionalism in the Arts," pp. 65–101 · "Federation or Disunion: The Political Economy of Regionalism," pp. 102–128 · "Still Rebels, Still Yankees," pp. 131–154 · "New York and the Hinterland," pp. 155–168 · "The Two Old Wests," pp. 169–191 · "The Great Plains," pp. 192–211 · "American Heroes," pp. 212–227 · "Regionalism and Nationalism in American Literature," pp. 228–239 · "Regionalism and Education," pp. 240–257 · "The Dilemma of the Southern Liberals," pp. 261–284 · "Howard Odum and the Sociological Proteus," pp. 285–311 · "Expedients Vs. Principles—Cross-Purposes in the South," pp. 312–338 · "The Southern Poet and His Tradition," pp. 339–346 · "The Shape of Things and Men: H. G. Wells and Æ on the World State," pp. 349–368.

Signed Reviews

AGAR, HERBERT. *Saturday Review of Literature,* XVII (April 23, 1938), 16.
ANDERSON, EUGENE. Macon *Telegraph,* May 14, 1938.
BEATTY, RICHMOND CROOM. Nashville *Banner,* March 19, 1938.
DINKINS, HARVEY. Winston-Salem *Sentinel,* March 13, 1938.
DYER, J. P. Savannah *News,* April 3, 1938.
FRIERSON, WILLIAM C. Birmingham *News-Age-Herald,* May 1, 1938.

Gaus, J. M. *American Political Science Review,* XXXII (December, 1938), 1180.

Hill, Helen. *Virginia Quarterly Review,* XIV (Autumn, 1938), 613–617.

Hoagland, Clayton. New York *Sun,* April 15, 1938.

Jenckes, E. N. Springfield *Republican,* March 5, 1938.

Jones, D. Dallas *Morning News,* May 22, 1938.

Meacham, William Shands. *Survey Graphic,* XXVIII (January, 1939), 37.

Miller, Francis Pickens. Roanoke *World News,* July 3, 1938. Reprinted Virginia Beach *News,* July 15, 1938.

Moore, Harry Estill, *Social Forces,* XVII (December, 1938), 281–282.

Prescott, Frank W. Chattanooga *Sunday Times Magazine,* May 3, 1938.

Reynolds, Horace. *Christian Science Monitor Magazine Section,* July 6, 1938, p. 10.

Robison, Dan M. *Vanderbilt Alumnus,* XXIII (May, 1938), 8.

Tate, Allen. Raleigh *News and Observer,* March 13, 1938.

Thompson, John. Nashville *Tennessean,* April 3, 1938.

Unsigned Reviews

Durham *Morning Herald,* March 20, 1938.

Knoxville *Journal,* March 27, 1938.

London *Times Literary Supplement,* XXXVII (August 20, 1938), 547

Montgomery *Advertiser* (R.F.H., Jr.), March 27, 1938.

Savannah *Press,* June 25, 1938. Reprinted Charlotte *Observer,* June 26, 1938.

The Attack on Leviathan. Regionalism and Nationalism in the United States. Gloucester, Mass.: Peter Smith, 1962.
Reprint of above.

Review

Kirk, Russell. *National Review,* XIV (June 18, 1963), 498.

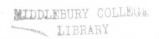

Lee in the Mountains and Other Poems Including The Tall Men.
(Poems.) Boston and New York: Houghton Mifflin Company,
1938.

Contents

"Lee in the Mountains," pp. 3–7 · "Aunt Maria and the
Gourds," pp. 8–10 · "The Last Charge," pp. 11–14 · "The
Deserter: A Christmas Eclogue," pp. 15–22 · "The Running of
Streight," pp. 23–35 · "Two Georgia Pastorals" · "Old Black
Joe Comes Home," pp. 36–38 · "Randall, My Son," p. 39 ·
"From a Chimney Corner," pp. 40–41 · "Sequel of Appomat-
tox," pp. 42–43 · "The Last Rider," pp. 44–45 · "Southward
Returning," pp. 46–47 · "Assembly at Murfreesboro," pp. 48–
49 · "On a Replica of the Parthenon," pp. 50–51 · "Twilight
on Union Street," p. 52 · "The Horde," pp. 53–54 · "Sanctuary," pp. 55–58 · "Prologue: The Long Street," pp. 63–64 ·
"The Tall Men," pp. 65–74 · "The Sod of Battle-Fields," pp.
75–82 · "Geography of the Brain," pp. 83–93 · "The Faring,"
pp. 94–108 · "Conversation in a Bedroom," pp. 109–119 ·
"The Breaking Mould," pp. 120–126 · "Epithalamion," pp.
127–133 · "Epilogue: Fire on Belmont Street," pp. 134–137.

Signed Reviews

AMES, KATHRYN. Winston-Salem *Sentinel,* October 16, 1938.

BEATTY, RICHMOND CROOM. *Vanderbilt Alumnus,* XXIV (November, 1938), 9–10.

BERRYMAN, JOHN. New York *Herald Tribune Books,* January
8, 1939, p. 12.

CAMERON, KENNETH. Macon *Telegraph,* December 25, 1938.

DORRANCE, WARD ALLISON. Columbia *Missourian,* January 14,
1939.

FRIERSON, WILLIAM C. Birmingham *News-Age-Herald,* January
8, 1939.

HOLMES, JOHN. Boston *Transcript,* October 19, 1938.

JACK, PETER MONRO. New York *Times Book Review,* March 19,
1939, p. 9.

LOGAN, FLOYD. Fort Wayne *News-Sentinel,* November 28, 1938.

MILLSPAUGH, C. A. *Poetry,* LIV (May, 1939), 108–111.
MORRISON, THEODORE. *Atlantic Monthly,* CLXIII (February, 1939), [page unnumbered].
O'DONNELL, GEORGE MARION. Memphis *Commercial Appeal,* January 1, 1939.
PALMER, ELIZABETH C. Chattanooga *Times,* November 20, 1938.
STOKES, ELSIE WARREN. Nashville *Observer,* October 28, 1938.
THOMPSON, JOHN. Nashville *Tennessean,* October 16, 1938.
ZABEL, MORTON DAUWEN. *Southern Review,* V (Winter, 1940), 582–583.

Unsigned Reviews

Atlanta *Journal,* October 30, 1938.
Kansas City *Star* (W.A.D.), January 7, 1939.
Nation, CXLVII (December 10, 1938), 637.
North American Review, CCXLVI (Winter, 1938–1939), 407.
Springfield *Republican* (A.M.J.), February 12, 1939.
Time, XXXII (December 26, 1938), 43–44.
Washington *Star,* October 30, 1938.

Lee in the Mountains and Other Poems Including The Tall Men. New York: Charles Scribner's Sons, 1949.
Reissue of above.

Review

McGINLEY, PHYLLIS. New York *Times Book Review,* July 31, 1949, p. 5.

American Composition and Rhetoric. (Textbook.) New York: Charles Scribner's Sons, 1939.

American Composition and Rhetoric. New York: Charles Scribner's Sons, 1943.
Reissue of above.

American Composition and Rhetoric. Revised Edition in Collaboration with Ivar Lou Myhr. New York: Charles Scribner's Sons, 1947.

American Composition and Rhetoric. Third Edition. New York: Charles Scribner's Sons, 1953.

American Composition and Rhetoric. Fourth Edition. New York: Charles Scribner's Sons, 1959.

Reviews

FLEISCHAUER, WARREN A. *The University Bookman,* I (Autumn, 1960), 15–22.
SHERWOOD, JOHN C. *College English,* XXI (April, 1960), 427.

Concise American Composition and Rhetoric. New York: Charles Scribner's Sons, 1964.
Paperback condensation and revision of above.

Readings for Composition From Prose Models. (Textbook.) Edited in collaboration with Sidney Erwin Glenn. New York: Charles Scribner's Sons, 1942.

Readings for Composition From Prose Models. Second Edition. Edited in collaboration with Sidney Erwin Glenn. New York: Charles Scribner's Sons, 1957.

Review

FLEISCHAUER, WARREN A. *The University Bookman,* I (Autumn, 1960), 15–22.

The Tennessee. Volume I: The Old River, Frontier to Secession. Illustrated by Theresa Sherrer Davidson. New York and Toronto: Rinehart & Company, 1946. (The Rivers of America Series.)

Signed Reviews

BAUER, FRANK. Hartford *Times,* November 9, 1946.
BOLMAN, HELEN P. *Library Journal,* LXXI (October 15, 1946), 1461–1462.
COLBURN, HELEN. *Augusta* (Ga.) *Chronicle,* December 1, 1946.
CRAVEN, AVERY. New York *Herald Tribune Weekly Book Review,* October 27, 1946, p. 4.
DICKINSON, S. D. Little Rock *Gazette,* November 10, 1946.

Douglas, Mary Stahlman. Nashville *Banner,* November 20, 1946.

Duncan, Alderman. Columbia (S.C.) *State,* November 3, 1946.

Folmsbee, Stanley J. *Journal of Southern History,* XIII (February, 1947), 110–112.

Frederick, J. T. The Chicago *Sun Book Week,* October 20, 1946, p. 2.

Gould, Ray. Montgomery *Advertiser,* February 9, 1947.

Havighurst, Walter. Chicago *Tribune,* October 27, 1946.

Hoagland, Clayton. New York *Sun,* October 23, 1946.

Hoover, Gladys. San Jose *Mercury Herald,* December 15, 1946.

Kiessling, E. C. Milwaukee *Journal,* October 27, 1946.

Kroll, Harry Harrison. New York *Times Book Review,* December 8, 1946, p. 26.

Reynolds, Horace. *Christian Science Monitor,* November 20, 1946.

Sessions, Al. Richmond (Cal.) *Contra Costa Labor Journal,* November 22, 1946.

Strickland, Rex W. Dallas *Times-Herald,* December 22, 1946.

Voiles, Jane. San Francisco *Chronicle,* December 1, 1946.

Wilson, William E. Providence *Journal,* December 8, 1946.

Unsigned Reviews

Bakersfield *Californian,* November 23, 1946.

Boston *Traveler* (F.L.B.), December 2, 1946.

Charleston (S.C.) *News* (K.R.), December 22, 1946.

Chicago *News,* October 30, 1946.

Cincinnati *Times-Star,* November 11, 1946.

Kirkus, XIV (August 15, 1946), 412.

Los Angeles *Times* (P.J.S.), November 17, 1946.

New Orleans *Times-Picayune,* November 24, 1946.

United States Quarterly Book List, IV (September, 1948), 316.

Virginia Quarterly Review, XXIII (Spring, 1947), lviii.

The Tennessee. Volume II: The New River, Civil War to TVA. Illustrated by Theresa Sherrer Davidson. New York and Toronto: Rinehart & Company, 1948. (The Rivers of America Series.)

Signed Reviews

BARMANN, GEORGE J. Cleveland *Plain Dealer,* January 25, 1948.

BIRCHFIELD, JAMES. Washington *Star,* February 8, 1948.

BOATNER, MAXINE TULL. Hartford *Courant,* August 22, 1948.

CLARK, THOMAS D. *Southern Folklore Quarterly,* XII (March, 1948), 108–109.

DERLETH, AUGUST. Chicago *Tribune,* February 8, 1948.

DUNCAN, ALDERMAN. Columbia (S.C.) *Record,* February 12, 1948.

F[LOWERS], P[AUL]. Memphis *Commercial Appeal,* February 1, 1948.

FOLMSBEE, STANLEY J. *Journal of Southern History,* XIV (May, 1948), 281–284.

GREENE, LEE S. *Public Administration Review,* IX (Autumn, 1949), 294–297.

HOAGLAND, CLAYTON. New York *Sun,* January 26, 1948.

HODGES, LEIGH MITCHELL. Philadelphia *Bulletin,* January 18, 1948.

JOHNSON, GERALD W. New York *Herald Tribune Weekly Book Review,* January 25, 1948, pp 1–2.

KIRSCHTEN, ERNEST. *Nation.* CLXVI (April 17, 1948), 421.

LYONS, HILARY. *Holiday,* III (April, 1948), 151.

McDONALD, GERALD D. *Library Journal,* LXXII (December 15, 1947), 1776.

McGINNIS, JOHN H. Dallas *News,* February 29, 1948.

NIXON, H.C. *American Political Science Review,* XLII (June, 1948), 596–597.

PEASE, HARRY. Milwaukee *Journal,* February 1, 1948.

REYNOLDS, HORACE. New York *Times Book Review,* January 25, 1948, p. 24.

SEARS, WILLIAM P. *Education,* LXIX (February, 1949), 387.

SMITH, CULVER H. *American Historical Review,* LIV (January, 1949), 449–450.

TERRAL, RUFUS. St. Louis *Post-Dispatch,* February 15, 1948.

WHITMAN, WILLSON. *Saturday Review of Literature,* XXXI January 31, 1948), 17.

Unsigned Reviews

Christian Science Monitor Magazine Section (R.M.H.), May 15, 1948, p. 12.
Current History, XV (July, 1948), 40.
Kirkus, XV (November 15, 1947), 639.
New Orleans *Times-Picayune* (J.I.), May 2, 1948.
New Yorker, XXIII (January 24, 1948), 86.
Providence *Journal* (K.B.R.), May 16, 1948.
United States Quarterly Book List, IV (September, 1948), 316.
Virginia Quarterly Review, XXIV (Summer, 1948), lxxvi–lxxvii.

Twenty Lessons in Reading and Writing Prose. (Textbook.) New York: Charles Scribner's Sons, 1955.

Still Rebels, Still Yankees and Other Essays. (Essays.) Wood Engraving [Frontispiece] by Theresa Sherrer Davidson. Baton Rouge: Louisiana State University Press, 1957.

Contents

"Poetry as Tradition," pp. 3–22 · "Yeats and the Centaur," pp. 23–30 · "In Memory of John Gould Fletcher," pp. 31–40 · "The Traditional Basis of Thomas Hardy's Fiction," pp. 43–61 · "Futurism and Archaism in Toynbee and Hardy," pp. 62–83 · "Theme and Method in *So Red the Rose,*" pp. 84–101 · "The Tradition of Irreverence," pp. 105–127 · "Current Attitudes toward Folklore," pp. 128–136 · "The Sacred Harp in the Land of Eden," pp. 137–151 · "The Origins of Our Heroes," pp. 152–156 · "Why the Modern South Has a Great Literature," pp. 159–179 · "In Justice to So Fine a Country," pp. 180–190 · "Mr. Cash and the Proto-Dorian South," pp. 191–212 · "Some Day, in Old Charleston," pp. 213–227 · "Still Rebels, Still Yankees," pp. 231–253 · "New York and the Hinterland," pp. 254–266 · "Regionalism and Nationalism in American Literature," pp. 267–278.

Signed Reviews

ALDRIDGE, JOHN W. New York *Times Book Review,* May 5, 1957, p. 4.

BLACKFORD, FRANK. Norfolk *Pilot,* April 28, 1957.

CARTER, THOMAS H. *Shenandoah,* IX (Winter, 1958), 45–53.

CHENEY, BRAINARD. Nashville *Banner,* April 26, 1957.

COHEN, HENNIG. *Journal of Southern History,* XXIII (August, 1957), 404–405.

COWAN, LOUISE. *New Mexico Quarterly,* XXVII (Spring, Summer, 1957), 136–138.

DOWDEY, CLIFFORD. Richmond (Va.) *Times Dispatch,* June 2, 1957.

DRAKE, ROBERT Y. *Modern Age,* II (Winter, 1957–1958), 94–96.

FLOWERS, PAUL. Memphis *Commercial Appeal,* April 7, 1957.

FOGLE, RICHARD HARTER. *College English,* XIX (March, 1958), 278.

HESSELTINE, WILLIAM B. Jackson (Tenn.) *Sun,* July 7, 1957.

HUBBELL, JAY B. *South Atlantic Quarterly,* LVI (Autumn, 1957), 525–527.

KENNY, MARGARET. *American,* XCVII (August 3, 1957), 469.

LONN, ELLA. *Annals of the American Academy of Political and Social Science,* CCCXIII (September, 1957), 157.

LUTES, VIRGIL C. *Library Journal,* LXXXII (April 1, 1957), 978.

PRITCHARD, J. P. Oklahoma City *Oklahoman,* July 7, 1957.

REAVER, J. RUSSEL. *Midwest Folklore,* VIII (Winter, 1958), 224–225.

REDMAN, BEN RAY. Chicago *Tribune,* April 28, 1957.

RUBIN, LOUIS D., JR. Baltimore *Sun,* March 21, 1957.

STEWART, RANDALL. *New England Quarterly,* XXX (June, 1957), 260–262.

STOKELY, WILMA DYKEMAN. Chattanooga *Times,* July 20, 1957.

WALSER, RICHARD. *North Carolina Historical Review,* XXXIV (October, 1957), 555–556.

WATTS, CHARLES H., II. Providence *Journal,* April 28, 1957.

WEAVER, RICHARD M. Nashville *Tennessean,* April 14, 1957.

WINTERICH, JOHN T. *Saturday Review,* XL (May 4, 1957), 50.

YOUNG, STARK. *Georgia Review,* XI (Summer, 1957), 227–229.

Unsigned Review

Raleigh *Observer,* June 9, 1957.

Southern Writers in the Modern World. Eugenia Dorothy Blount Lamar Memorial Lectures, 1957. Delivered at Mercer University on November 20 and 21. Athens: University of Georgia Press, 1958.

Contents

"The Thankless Muse and Her Fugitive Poets," pp. 1–30 · "Counterattack, 1930–1940: The South Against Leviathan," pp. 31–62 · "The Southern Writer and the Modern University," pp. 63–76.

Signed Reviews

Bulgin, Randolph M. *Shenandoah,* XI (Autumn, 1959), 35–37.

Cheney, Frances Neel. Nashville *Banner,* September 7, 1958.

Drake, Robert Y. *Modern Age,* III (Spring, 1959), 203–206.

England, Kenneth. *Georgia Review,* XIII (Summer, 1959), 233–234.

Govan, Gilbert E. Chattanooga *Times,* July 6, 1958.

Hicks, Granville. *Saturday Review,* XLI (June 21, 1958), 50.

May, James Boyer. *Trace,* No. 33 (August-September, 1959), 35–36.

Rubin, Louis D. *Journal of Southern History,* XXV (February, 1959), 140–142.

Thompson, Frank H. *Prairie Schooner,* XXXIII (Fall, 1959), 281–283.

Walser, Richard. *South Atlantic Quarterly,* LVIII (Winter, 1959), 128.

Ward, C. Anne. *New Mexico Quarterly,* XXVIII (Summer, Autumn, Winter, 1958), 183–185.

Weaver, Richard M. Nashville *Tennessean,* July 13, 1958.

Unsigned Review

Virginia Quarterly Review, XXXIV (Autumn, 1958), cxiv.

The Long Street. Poems. (Poems.) Engravings by Theresa Sherrer Davidson. Nashville: Vanderbilt University Press, 1961.

Contents

"The Ninth Part of Speech," pp. 3–7 · "Gradual of the Northern Summer," pp. 8–11 · "A Barren Look," p. 12 · "A Touch of Snow," pp. 13–14 · "Late Answer: A Civil War Seminar," pp. 15–17 · "Lines Written for Allen Tate on His Sixtieth Anniversary," pp. 21–22 · "Soldier and Son," pp. 23–24 · "Woodlands, 1956–60," pp. 25–27 · "Hermitage," pp. 28–30 · "Old Sailor's Choice," pp. 31–36 · "Meditation on Literary Fame," p. 37 · "The Nervous Man," pp. 38–39 · "At the Station," p. 40 · "Relic of the Past," p. 41 · "Handicaps I," p. 42 · "Handicaps II," p. 43 · "Handicaps III," p. 44 · "Joe Clisby's Song," pp. 47–48 · "On Culleoka Road," p. 49 · "Second Harvest," p. 50 · "The Swinging Bridge," p. 51 · "Spring Voices," p. 52 · "Crabbed Youth and Merry Age," p. 53 · "Country Roses: A Song," p. 54 · "The Case of Motorman 17: Commitment Proceedings," pp. 57–70 · "Apple and Mole," p. 73 · "Martha and Shadow," p. 74 · "Wild Game," p. 75 · "Cross Section of a Landscape," p. 76 · "Litany," p. 77 · "Prelude in a Garden," p. 78 · "Pavane," p. 79 · "The Roman Road," p. 80 · "Stone and Roses," p. 81 · "Fiddler Dow," pp. 82–85 · "The Old Man of Thorn," pp. 86–88 · "Spoken at a Castle Gate," pp. 89–90.

Reviews

COOLEY, FRANKLIN D. Richmond *Times Dispatch,* November 12, 1961.

COWAN, LOUISE. *Georgia Review,* XVI (Summer, 1962), 226–229.

DAPONTE, DURANT. *Southern Observer,* VIII (November, 1961), 173–174.

DAVIS, PAXTON. Roanoke *Times,* October 15, 1961.

DEFORD, MAEBELLE ASHWORTH. Columbus (Ga.) *Enquirer,* October 16, 1961.

DICKEY, JAMES. New York *Times Book Review,* December 24, 1961, pp. 4–5.

DONNELLY, DOROTHY. *Poetry,* C (September, 1962), 395–400.

DRAKE, ROBERT. *Christian Century,* LXXVIII (December 27, 1961), 1561.

ENGLAND, KENNETH. Nashville *Tennessean,* October 22, 1961.

GORLIER, CLAUDIO. *L'Approdo Letterario,* Anno VIII, No. 17–18 (1962), 209–212. (In Italian.)

HALL, BARBARA HODGE. Anniston *Star,* October 15, 1961.

HAZO, SAMUEL. *Commonweal,* LXXV (December 22, 1961), 346.

JACOBSON, JOSEPHINE. Baltimore *Evening Sun,* January 22, 1962.

KIRK, RUSSELL. *National Review,* XIII (July 17, 1962), 25.

KOHLER, DAYTON. Louisville *Courier-Journal,* April 8, 1962.

MAY, JAMES BOYER. *Trace,* No. 45 (Spring, 1962), 151–153.

MEACHAM, HARRY M. Richmond *News Leader,* December 6, 1961.

MYRICK, SUSAN. Macon *Telegraph,* October 19, 1961.

NOLAN, JAMES W. New Orleans *Times-Picayune,* January 21, 1962.

O'CONNOR, WILLIAM VAN. *Saturday Review,* XLV (January 6, 1962), 70.

RANSOM, JOHN CROWE. *Sewanee Review,* LXX (Spring, 1962), 202–207.

RIPPY, FRANCES MAYHEW. Beaumont *Journal,* September 7, 1962.

STEWART, JAMES T. *South Carolina Librarian,* VI (1962), 16–17.

TATE, ALLEN. *Sewanee Review,* LXX (Autumn, 1962), 671–673.

WADE, JOHN DONALD. *Sewanee Review,* LXX (Spring, 1962), 208–212.

WELKER, ROBERT L. Nashville *Banner,* October 20, 1961.

WILLIAMS, MILLER. Baton Rouge *Advocate,* February 25, 1962.

WILSON, JAMES SOUTHALL. *Virginia Quarterly Review,* XXXVIII (Spring, 1962), 330–332.

The Spyglass. Views and Reviews, 1924–1930. [Book Reviews and Essays.] Selected and Edited by John Tyree Fain. Nashville: Vanderbilt University Press, 1963.

Contents

"Provincialism," pp. 3–7 · "T. S. Stribling," pp. 11–16 · "Elizabeth Madox Roberts," pp. 16–20 · "Julia Peterkin," pp. 20–23 · "Conrad Aiken," pp. 23–26 · "Frances Newman," pp. 26–29 · "An Author Divided Against Himself" [DuBose Heyward], pp. 29–34 · "Stark Young and Others," pp. 34–39 · "Farewell—and Hail!" [Cabell and Wolfe], pp. 40–44 · "Elizabeth Madox Roberts," pp. 44–48 · "Ellen Glasgow—Social Historian," pp. 49–53 · "Roark Bradford," pp. 53–55 · "Glenway Wescott, *The Apple of the Eye*," pp. 59–60 · "Sherwood Anderson's *A Story Teller's Story*," pp. 61–63 · "Sinclair Lewis," pp. 63–67 · "Theodore Dreiser," pp. 67–70 · "Edna Ferber," pp. 70–74 · "Tragedy of Limitation: Tarkington and Hemingway," pp. 75–79 · "Mr. Nicholson's Jackson," pp. 79–82 · "Irony: Edith Wharton, Louis Bromfield," pp. 83–87 · "Perfect Behavior" [Ernest Hemingway], pp. 88–92 · "Painful Literature" [Julian Green], pp. 93–95 · "John Masefield," pp. 99–102 · "Thomas Hardy," pp. 102–104 · "John Crowe Ransom," p. 105 · "Hart Crane's *White Buildings*," pp. 106–109 · "The Gumdrop School" [*Journal of American Poetry*], pp. 109–110 · "Josephine Pinckney, *Sea-Drinking Cities*," pp. 111–113 · "Carl Sandburg," pp. 114–115 · "Elinor Wylie," pp. 115–117 · "Harriet Monroe," pp. 121–125 · "H. L. Mencken," pp. 126–131 · "Two Professors" [V. L. Parrington and J. L. Lowes], pp. 131–137 · "Two Critics" [H. S. Canby and T. S. Eliot], pp. 137–142 · "Notes" [Stanley Johnson, John Crowe Ransom, and miscellaneous], pp. 145–148 · "Note" [Polish authors], p. 148 · "Notes: Sex in Literature, Poetry Magazines," pp. 149–152 · "Notes: Zona Gale, Censorship," pp. 153–158 · "Old Songs" [Ballads] pp. 158–161 · "Crippled Caravan" [*Second American Caravan*], pp. 161–163 · "Book Clubs," pp. 164–167 · "Notes: Reviewing, Thornton Wilder, Elinor Wylie," pp. 167–169 · "The Amateur Spirit in Music" [D. G. Mason's *Dilemma of American Music*], pp. 170–175 · "Prose Style, *Blues* Magazine," pp. 175–178 · "Book-of-the-Month Club," pp. 178–180 · "Antiques, Handcraft" [H. H. Taylor's *Knowing, Collecting and Restoring Early*

American Furniture], pp. 180–183 · "The Book Business" [R. L. Duffus's *Books: Their Place in a Democracy*], pp. 184–188 · "Sassoon's War," pp. 188–193 · "Frank Lawrence Owsley," pp. 197–200 · "Stonewall Jackson's Way" [Allen Tate's *Stonewall Jackson: The Good Soldier*], pp. 201–206 · "The Spotlight on the South" [Howard Mumford Jones and John Crowe Ransom on the South], pp. 207–211 · "Phillips's *Life and Labor in the Old South*," pp. 211–217 · "Bower's *The Tragic Era*," pp. 217–224 · "What Does History Mean?", pp. 224–229 · "James Truslow Adams's *Our Business Civilization*, Ralph Borsodi's *This Ugly Civilization*," pp. 229–233 · "The World as Ford Factory," pp. 234–238 · "Criticism Outside New York," pp. 239–256.

Signed Reviews

BLUM, MORGAN. *Sewanee Review*, LXXI (Autumn, 1963), 690–691.

COLEMAN, DERO. Tulsa *World*, August 4, 1963.

CRITOPH, GERALD E. *American Quarterly*, XV (Winter, 1963), 595.

DAVENPORT, GUY. *National Review*, XVI (January 28, 1964), 79.

INGE, M. THOMAS. Nashville *Tennessean*, April 21, 1963.

KANE, KARL. Charleston (S.C.) *News and Courier*, April 28, 1963.

MAY, JAMES BOYER. *Trace*, No. 51 (Winter, 1963–1964), 341–343.

RUBIN, LOUIS D. *South Atlantic Quarterly*, LXIII (Spring, 1964), 245–246.

SCHLUETER, PAUL. *Christian Century*, LXXXI (March 25, 1964), 402.

THOMPSON, FRANCIS J. Roanoke *Times*, June 16, 1963.

Unsigned Reviews

Anniston *Star* (B.H.H.), April 21, 1963.

Journal of Southern History, XXIX (November, 1963), 548–549.

Virginia Quarterly Review, XXXIX (Autumn, 1963), cxxviii.

II. *Pamphlets*

Christmas in the Old South. A talk made by Mr. Donald Davidson of Vanderbilt University on the Caldwell radio program
December 21, 1928. No. 13. Caldwell & Company Southern
Securities, 400 Union Street, Nashville, Tenn. [A four-page
leaflet.]

A Study of the Honor System at Vanderbilt University. Donald
Davidson, Chairman. Nashville: Vanderbilt University, 1944.
[Edited and largely written by Davidson as Chairman of a
Faculty-Student Joint Committee.]

To the Warders of the Gate. A Memorandum on the Teaching
of Composition and Rhetoric—and of Almost Anything Else
That May Happen Along, Including Philosophy, History,
Logic, Spelling, Footnotes, Etiquette, the Literary Arts, Philol-
ogy, Punctuation, the Dewey Decimal System, and the Ein-
stein Formula. New York: Charles Scribner's Sons, 1948. [A
prospectus for *American Composition and Rhetoric,* Revised
Edition (1947), and *Readings for Composition From Prose
Models* (1942).]

Tyranny at Oak Ridge. An Account of How "Integration" was
forced upon certain Public Schools in disregard of the Laws,
Customs, and Educational Policies of the State of Tennessee
and despite the Protests of Citizens; how "Integration" by
FEDERAL FIAT has affected the Educational and other
arrangements at Oak Ridge; and a Narrative of Events in
Anderson County and East Tennessee. Nashville: The Tennessee Federation for Constitutional Government, 1956. [An
unsigned pamphlet written by Davidson as State Chairman

of the Tennessee Federation for Constitutional Government.]

The Crisis in Tennessee. A Message to the Members of the General Assembly of the State of Tennessee Containing Proposals for Legislative Action to Preserve the State Educational System and to Safeguard and Maintain the Sovereign Rights of the State of Tennessee and Its People. Prepared and Distributed by the Tennessee Federation for Constitutional Government. [An unsigned pamphlet written by Davidson as State Chairman of the Tennessee Federation for Constitutional Government. 1957.]

To See Through All Things. A Coffee House Club Poem. December 17, 1964. Nashville: Coffee House Club, 1964. [A limited edition of a ninety-five line poem prepared especially for the membership of the Coffee House Club of Nashville.]

III. *Poems*

"A Barren Look," *The Long Street,* p. 12.

"A Dead Romanticist," *Fugitive,* I (October, 1922), 85. *An Outland Piper,* p. 31.

"A Demon Brother," *Fugitive,* I (April, 1922), 6–7. *An Outland Piper* (as "An Outland Piper"), pp. 3–5, Addison Hibbard, ed., *The Lyric South* (New York: The Macmillan Company, 1928), pp. 223–224.

"A Touch of Snow," *The Long Street,* pp. 13–14.

"Afternoon Call," *Folio* (1923), [page unnumbered]. *An Outland Piper,* pp. 52–53. Addison Hibbard, ed., *The Lyric South* (New York: The Macmillan Company, 1928), pp. 182–183.

"All Fools' Calendar," *Voices,* V (January, 1926), 133. William Stanley Braithwaite, ed., *Anthology of Magazine Verse for 1926* (Boston: B. J. Brimmer, 1926), pp. 109–110. *Voices,* No. 146 (1951), 35–36.

"Alla Stoccata," *Fugitive,* II (August-September, 1923), 115–117. *An Outland Piper,* pp. 59–63.

"An Outland Piper," see "A Demon Brother."

"Apple and Mole," see "Not Long Green."

"Assembly at Murfreesboro," *Lee in the Mountains,* pp. 48–49.

"At the Station," *The Long Street,* p. 40.

"Aunt Maria and the Gourds," *Poetry,* XL (May, 1932), 76–78. *Lee in the Mountains,* pp. 8–10.

"Avalon," *Fugitive,* II (June-July, 1922), 80–81. *Armageddon* by John Crowe Ransom, The Southern Prize Poem and the Honors of 1923 (Charleston: The Poetry Society of South

Carolina, 1923), pp. 14–16. *An Outland Piper*, pp. 41–43. *Fugitives, An Anthology of Verse* (New York: Harcourt, Brace and Company, 1928), pp. 12–13. Addison Hibbard, ed., *The Lyric South* (New York: The Macmillan Company, 1928), pp. 225–226.

"Boundary," *Fugitive*, IV (March, 1925), 12.

"Bryony," *The Reviewer*, V (April, 1925), 100.

"By Due Process," *Fugitive*, III (August, 1924), 119–121.

"Censored," *Fugitive*, I (October, 1922), 91. *An Outlined Piper*, p. 72.

"Competition," *An Outland Piper*, pp. 70–71.

"Conversation in a Bedroom," *The Tall Men*, pp. 68–85. *Lee in the Mountains*, pp. 109–119.

"Corymba," *The Double Dealer*, IV (October, 1922), 187–188. *An Outland Piper*, pp. 32–34. *Fugitives, An Anthology of Verse* (New York: Harcourt, Brace and Company, 1928), pp. 10–11.

"Country Roses: A Song," *The Long Street*, p. 54.

"Crabbed Youth and Merry Age," *The Quill*, VI (Spring, 1934), 10. *The Long Street*, p. 53.

"Cross Section of a Landscape," *Fugitive*, IV (March, 1925), 14. Louis Untermeyer, ed., *Modern American Poetry*, Third Revised Edition (New York: Harcourt, Brace and Company, 1925), p. 537; Fourth Revised Edition (1930), p. 677; Fifth Revised Edition (1936), pp. 515–516; Sixth Revised Edition (1942), p. 538. *Fugitives, An Anthology of Verse* (New York: Harcourt, Brace and Company, 1928), p. 14. *Vanderbilt Masquerader*, X (December, 1933), 11. *The Long Street*, p. 76.

"Drums and Brass," *Fugitive*, II (June-July, 1923), 69. William Stanley Braithwaite, ed., *Anthology of Magazine Verse for 1923* (Boston: B. J. Brimmer Company, 1923), pp. 82–83. *An Outland Piper*, pp. 29–30. *Fugitives, An Anthology of Verse* (New York: Harcourt, Brace and Company, 1928), pp. 8–9.

"Dryad," *The Double Dealer*, IV (October, 1922), 188. *The Yearbook of the Poetry Society of South Carolina*, II (1924), 22. *An Outland Piper*, pp. 35–36.

"Earthbound," *The Yearbook of the Poetry Society of South Carolina*, III (1927), 34.

"Ecclesiasticus," *Fugitive*, II (February-March, 1923), 23. William Stanley Braithwaite, ed., *Anthology of Magazine Verse for 1923* (Boston: B. J. Brimmer Company, 1923), pp. 80–81. *An Outland Piper* (as "Ecclesiasticus I"), pp. 64–65. Addison Hibbard, ed., *The Lyric South* (New York: The Macmillan Company, 1928), pp. 128–129.

"Ecclesiasticus II," *An Outland Piper*, pp. 66–67.

"Epithalamion," *The Tall Men*, pp. 96–105. Jessie B. Rittenhouse, ed., *The Third Book of Modern Verse* (Boston and New York: Houghton Mifflin Company, 1927), pp. 320–321 [reprints only the concluding thirty-three lines]. *Lee in the Mountains*, pp. 127–133.

"Fear in a Cubicle," *Fugitive*, IV (March, 1925), 13.

"Fiddler Dow," *Fugitive*, III (April, 1924), 60–62. *The Long Street*, pp. 82–85.

"Fire on Belmont Street," *The Yearbook of the Poetry Society of South Carolina*, II (1926), 23–25. *The Tall Men*, pp. 113–117. *Fugitives, An Anthology of Verse* (New York: Harcourt, Brace and Company, 1928), pp. 3–6. Louis Untermeyer, ed., *Modern American Poetry*, Fourth Revised Edition (New York: Harcourt, Brace and Company, 1930), pp. 678–680; Fifth Revised Edition (1936), pp. 517–518; Sixth Revised Edition (1942), pp. 539–541. *Vanderbilt Masquerader*, X (December, 1933), 10–11. Edd Winfield Parks, ed., *Southern Poets* (New York: American Book Company, 1936), pp. 289–292. *Lee in the Mountains*, pp. 134–137.

"Following the Tiger," *Fugitive*, I (April, 1922), 17–19. *An Outland Piper*, pp. 24–26.

"For Example," *Fugitive*, IV (June, 1925), 46–47.

"From a Chimney Corner," *Lee in the Mountains*, pp. 40–41.

"Geography of the Brain," *The Tall Men*, pp. 28–43. *Lee in the Mountains*, pp. 83–93.

"Gradual of the Northern Summer," *The Long Street*, pp. 8–11.

"Handicaps I," *The Long Street*, p. 42.

"Handicaps II," *The Long Street*, p. 43.

"Handicaps III," *The Long Street*, p. 44

"Hermitage," *Virginia Quarterly Review*, XIX (Winter, 1943), 65–67. *The Long Street*, pp 28–30. William Pratt, ed., *The Fugitive Poets* (New York: E. P. Dutton and Company, 1965), pp. 84–87.

"Hit or Miss," *Fugitive*, IV (December, 1925), 100–101.

"Iconoclast," *Fugitive*, II (February-March, 1923), 5. *An Outland Piper*, pp. 68–69.

"Jasper," *Palms*, II (Midsummer, 1924), 37. William Stanley Braithwaite, ed., *Anthology of Magazine Verse for 1925* (Boston: B. J. Brimmer Company, 1925), p. 95.

"Joe Clisby's Song," *Georgia Review*, XIV (Spring, 1960), 35–36. *The Long Street*, pp. 47–48.

"John Darrow," *Fugitive*, II (February-March, 1923), 28–29. William Stanley Braithwaite, ed., *Anthology of Magazine Verse for 1923* (Boston: B. J. Brimmer Company, 1923), pp. 81–82. *An Outlined Piper*, pp. 19–21. Burton Egbert Stevenson, ed., *The Home Book of Modern Verse* (New York: Henry Holt and Company, 1925), pp. 660–662.

"Late Answer: A Civil War Seminar," *The Long Street*, pp. 15–17.

"Lee in the Mountains," *American Review*, III (May, 1934), 240–243. Edd Winfield Parks, ed., *Southern Poets* (New York: American Book Company, 1936), pp. 292–296. *Lee in the Mountains*, pp. 3–7. Cleanth Brooks, Jr., and Robert Penn Warren, *Understanding Poetry* (New York: Henry Holt and Company, 1938), pp. 517–520; Revised Complete Edition (1950), pp. 501–504; Third Edition (1960), pp. 476–479. Richmond Croom Beatty, ed., *A Vanderbilt Miscellany 1919–1944* (Nashville: Vanderbilt University Press, 1944), pp. 321–325. Edd Winfield Parks, ed., in collaboration with Olive Shaw and Michael Keller, *A Modern American Sampler*, Book II (Rio de Janeiro: Instituto Brasil—Estados Unidos, [1950]), pp. 214–217. Richmond Croom Beatty, Floyd C. Watkins, and Thomas Daniel Young, eds., *The Literature of the South* (Chicago: Scott, Foresman and Company, 1952), pp. 767–770. David Cecil and Allen Tate, eds., *Modern Verse in English*

1900–1950 (New York: The Macmillan Company, 1958), pp. 370–373. William Pratt, ed., *The Fugitive Poets* (New York: E. P. Dutton and Company, 1965), pp. 74–78. Translated into Italian by Claudio Gorlier, *Questioni,* Anno VIII (January-March, 1960), 56–60.

"Legend in Bronze," *Fugitive,* III (December, 1924), 137–140.

"Lines for a Tomb," *Fugitive,* IV (September, 1925), 80. L. A. G. Strong, ed., *The Best Poems of 1926* (New York: Dodd, Mead and Company, 1926), p. 43. William Pratt, ed., *The Fugitive Poets* (New York: E. P. Dutton and Company, 1965), p. 74.

"Lines Written for Allan Tate on His Sixtieth Anniversary," *Sewanee Review,* LXVII (Autumn, 1959), 540–541. *The Long Street,* pp. 21–22. William Pratt, ed., *The Fugitive Poets* (New York: E. P. Dutton and Company, 1965), pp. 87–88.

"Litany," *Fugitive,* II (December, 1923), 187. *Fugitives, An Anthology of Verse* (New York: Harcourt, Brace and Company, 1928), p. 7. *The Long Street,* p. 77.

"Martha and Shadow," *Nation,* CXXIII (August 18, 1926), 148. William Stanley Braithwaite, ed., *Anthology of Magazine Verse for 1927* (Boston: B. J. Brimmer Company, 1927), p. 82. *Fugitives, an Anthology of Verse* (New York: Harcourt, Brace and Company, 1928), p. 15. *The Long Street,* p. 74.

"Meditation on Literary Fame," *The Long Street,* p. 37.

"Naiad," *The Double Dealer,* IV (November, 1922), 216. *An Outline Piper,* pp. 39–40.

"Not Long Green," *Fugitive,* IV (June, 1925), 45. *Fugitives, An Anthology of Verse* (as "Apple and Mole") (New York: Harcourt, Brace and Company, 1928), p. 16. Louis Untermeyer, ed., *Modern American Poetry,* Fourth Revised Edition (New York: Harcourt, Brace and Company, 1930), pp. 680–681; Fifth Revised Edition (1936), p. 519; Sixth Revised Edition (1942), p. 541. *The Long Street,* p. 73.

"Old Black Joe Comes Home," *The Yearbook of the Poetry Society of Georgia,* X (1934), 17–19. *Lee in the Mountains,* pp. 36–38. *25th Anniversary: The Poetry Society of Georgia, 1923–1948* (Athens: University of Georgia Press, 1949), pp. 44–46.

"Old Harp," *Fugitive,* II (October, 1923), 133. *An Outland Piper,* pp. 6–7. *Sigma Upsilon News-Letter,* III (April 1, 1924), 1. Dallas *Morning News,* March 8, 1925, Part III, p. 5.

"Old Sailor's Choice," *The Long Street,* pp. 31–36.

"On a Replica of the Parthenon at Nashville," *Southern Review,* I (July, 1935), 83. *Lee in the Mountains,* pp. 50–51. Richmond Croom Beatty, ed., *A Vanderbilt Miscellany 1919–1940* (Nashville: Vanderbilt University Press, 1944), p. 326. David Cecil and Allen Tate, eds., *Modern Verse in English 1900–1950* (New York: The Macmillan Company, 1958), p. 373. William Pratt, ed., *The Fugitive Poets* (New York: E. P. Dutton and Company, 1965), p. 80.

"On Culleoka Road," *Georgia Review,* XIV (Spring, 1960), 36. *The Long Street,* p. 49.

"Palingenesis," *Fugitive,* III (June, 1924), 81.

"Pastorals Somewhat in the Modern Style: Echo, Advice to Shepherds, A Dirge," *Fugitive,* IV (December, 1925), 97–99.

"Pavane," *The Double Dealer,* V (May, 1923), 150. Edwin Markham, ed., *The Book of Poetry–American Poets,* 3 volumes (New York: William H. Wise and Company, 1926), p. 773; *The Book of American Poetry* (1934), p. 773; *Anthology of World's Best Poems* (1953), p. 773. *The Long Street,* p. 79.

"Portrait of a Wasp," *Fugitive,* IV (June, 1925), 48.

"Postscript of a Poor Scholar," *Fugitive,* I (December, 1922), 127. New York *Times Book Review,* January 14, 1923, p. 24. Nashville *Tennessean,* May 27, 1923, Special Feature Section, p. 1. *An Outland Piper,* p. 15.

"Pot Macabre," *Fugitive,* I (October, 1922), 82. *An Outland Piper,* pp. 73–74.

"Prelude in a Garden," *Fugitive,* III (April, 1924), 63. *The Long Street,* p. 78.

"Prie-Dieu," *Fugitive,* I (December, 1922), 102. *An Outland Piper,* pp. 44–45.

"Prisoner," *Palms,* I (Early, 1924), 177.

"Projection of a Body Upon Space," *Fugitive,* IV (September, 1925), 81.

"Randall My Son," *Lee in the Mountains,* p. 39. William Pratt, ed., *The Fugitive Poets* (New York: E. P. Dutton and Company, 1965), p. 81. Translated into Italian by Claudio Gorlier, *Questioni,* Anno VIII (January-March, 1960), 56–60.

"Redivivus," *Fugitive,* I (December, 1922), 109. *An Outland Piper,* p. 46. *Fugitives, An Anthology of Verse* (New York: Harcourt, Brace and Company, 1928), p. 17. Edd Winfield Parks, ed., *Southern Poets* (New York: American Book Company, 1936), p. 281. Edd Winfield Parks, ed., in collaboration with Olive Shaw and Michael Keller, *A Modern American Sampler,* Book II (Rio de Janeiro: Instituto Brasil—Estados Unidos, [1950]), p. 214.

"Refugees," W. Storrs Lee, ed., *Bread Loaf Anthology* (Middlebury, Vermont: Middlebury College Press, 1939), p. 53.

"Relic of the Past," *The Long Street,* p. 41.

"Requiescat," *Fugitive,* I (October, 1922), 79. *An Outland Piper,* pp. 47–48.

"Resurrection," *The Tall Men,* pp. 106–112.

"Sanctuary," *Lee in the Mountains,* pp. 55–58. Richmond Croom Beatty, ed., *A Vanderbilt Miscellany 1919–1944* (Nashville: Vanderbilt University Press, 1944), pp. 328–330. Richmond Croom Beatty, Floyd C. Watkins, and Thomas Daniel Young, eds., *The Literature of the South* (Chicago: Scott, Foresman and Company, 1952), pp. 770–772. William Pratt, ed., *The Fugitive Poets* (New York: E. P. Dutton and Company, 1965), pp. 82–84.

"Second Harvest," *The Long Street,* p. 50.

"Sequel of Appomattox," *Westminster Magazine,* XXIII (Winter, 1935), 253–254. *Lee in the Mountains,* pp. 42–43. William Pratt, ed., *The Fugitive Poets* (New York: E. P. Dutton and Company, 1965), pp. 78–79.

"Serenade," *Folio* (1923), [page unnumbered]. *An Outland Piper,* pp. 16–18.

"Soldier and Son," *The Long Street,* pp. 23–24.

"Song," *Sewanee Review,* XXXIII (October, 1925), 454.

"Southward Returning," *The Quill,* VI (Spring, 1934), 9. Edd Winfield Parks, ed., *Southern Poets* (New York: American Book Company, 1936), p. 292. *Lee in the Mountains,* pp. 46–47.

"Spoken at a Castle Gate," *The Measure*, No. 45 (November, 1924), 6. William Stanley Braithwaite, ed., *Anthology of Magazine Verse for 1925* (Boston: B. J. Brimmer Company, 1925), pp. 94–95. Louis Untermeyer, ed., *Modern American Poetry*, Third Revised Edition (New York: Harcourt, Brace and Company, 1925), pp. 537–539; Fourth Revised Edition (1930), pp. 677–678; Fifth Revised Edition (1936), p. 516; Sixth Revised Edition (1942), pp. 538–539. William Stanley Braithwaite and Margaret Haley Carpenter, eds., *Anthology of Magazine Verse for 1958* and *Anthology of Poems From the Seventeen Previously Published Braithwaite Anthologies* (New York: The Schulte Publishing Company, 1959), pp. 270–271. *The Long Street*, pp. 89–90.

"Spring Voices," *The Long Street*, p. 52.

"Stone and Roses," *Fugitive*, II (October, 1923), 138. *The Long Street*, p. 81.

"Sudden Meeting," *Fugitive*, IV (September, 1925), 79.

"Swan and Exile," *Fugitive*, III (June, 1924), 80.

"Teach Me," *Fugitive*, I (June, 1922), 40.

"The Amulet," *Fugitive*, I (October, 1922), 69. *An Outland Piper*, pp. 10–11.

"The Breaking Mould," *The Tall Men*, pp. 86–95. *Lee in the Mountains*, pp. 120–126.

"The Case of Motorman 17: Commitment Proceedings," *The Long Street*, pp. 57–70.

"The Deserter: A Christmas Eclogue," *Lee in the Mountains*, pp. 15–22.

"The Dragon Book," *Fugitive*, I (April, 1922), 13–14.

"The Faring," *The Tall Men*, pp. 44–67. *Lee in the Mountains*, pp. 94–108.

"The Horde," *Southern Review*, III (April, 1938), 790–791. *Lee in the Mountains*, pp. 53–54.

"The House of the Sun," *Fugitive*, I (June, 1922), 46. *An Outland Piper*, pp. 8–9.

"The Jester," *The Vanderbilt Observer*, XXXVII (June, 1915), 6.

"The Last Charge," *Lee in the Mountains*, pp. 11–14.

"The Last Rider," *Vanderbilt Masquerader*, X (December, 1933), 11. *Lee in the Mountains*, pp. 44–45.

"The Long Street," *The Tall Men*, pp. 1–3. *Lee in the Mountains*, pp. 63–64.

"The Man Who Would Not Die," *Fugitive*, II (April-May, 1923), 58–60. *An Outland Piper*, pp. 77–82.

"The Nervous Man," *Virginia Quarterly Review*, XXVI (Spring, 1950), pp. 214–215. Translated into Italian by Claudio Gorlier, *Questioni*, Anno VIII (January-March, 1960), 56–60. *The Long Street*, pp. 38–39.

"The Ninth Part of Speech," *Virginia Quarterly Review*, XXXVI (Autumn, 1960), 533–537. *The Long Street*, pp. 3–7.

"The Old Man of Thorn," *Fugitive*, III (February, 1924), 29–31. *The Long Street*, pp. 86–88.

"The Road to Mort-Homme," *Palms*, I (Autumn, 1923), 114. *An Outland Piper*, p. 54.

"The Roman Road," *The Long Street*, p. 80.

"The Running of Streight," *Lee in the Mountains*, pp. 23–25.

"The Sod of Battle-Fields," *The Tall Men*, pp. 18–27. *Lee in the Mountains*, pp. 75–82.

"The Swinging Bridge," *Fugitive*, II (June-July, 1923), 84. *The Long Street*, p. 51.

"The Tall Men," *The Tall Men*, pp. 4–17. Edd Winfield Parks, ed., *Southern Poets* (New York: American Book Company, 1936), pp. 281–289. *Lee in the Mountains*, pp. 65–74.

"The Tiger-Woman," *Fugitive*, I (June, 1922), 49–50. *An Outland Piper*, pp. 22–23. Stanton A. Coblentz, ed., *Modern American Lyrics* (New York: Minton, Balch & Company, 1924), pp. 176–177.

"The Valley of the Dragon," *Fugitive*, I (June, 1922), 36–37.

"The Wolf," *Fugitive*, II (August-September, 1923), 119. *An Outland Piper*, p. 51. Addison Hibbard, ed., *The Lyric South* (New York: The Macmillan Company, 1928), p. 227. Alfred Kreymborg, ed., *Lyric America* (New York: Coward-McCann, 1930), p. 525; *An Anthology of American Poetry*, Revised Edition (1935), p. 525; Second Revised Edition (1941), p. 525.

"To ———," *The Vanderbilt Observer*, XXXVII (February, 1915), 6.

"To One Who Could Not Understand," *Fugitive*, II (April-May, 1923), 55. *Sigma Upsilon News-Letter*, III (April 1, 1924), 1.

"Twilight Excursion," *The Double Dealer*, V (January, 1923), 36. *An Outland Piper*, pp. 37–38.

"Twilight on Union Street," *Lee in the Mountains*, p. 52. Harriet Marcelia Lucas, ed., *Prose and Poetry of Today, Regional America* (New York: The L. W. Singer Company, 1941), p. 112. Richmond Croom Beatty, ed., *A Vanderbilt Miscellany 1919–1940* (Nashville: Vanderbilt University Press, 1944), p. 327. William Pratt, ed., *The Fugitive Poets* (New York: E. P. Dutton and Company, 1965), p. 79.

"Two Georgia Pastorals," see "Old Black Joe Comes Home," and "Randall My Son."

"Utterance," *Fugitive*, II (October, 1923), 149. *An Outland Piper*, p. 55. Jessie B. Rittenhouse, ed., *The Third Book of Modern Verse* (New York: Houghton Mifflin Company, 1927), pp. 48–49. William Pratt, ed., *The Fugitive Poets* (New York: E. P. Dutton and Company, 1965), p. 73.

"Variation on an Old Theme," *Fugitive*, II (August-September, 1923), 102–103. *An Outland Piper*, pp. 12–14.

"Voice of the Dust," *Fugitive*, I (June, 1922), 56. *An Outland Piper*, pp. 49–50.

"When I Go Home," *The Vanderbilt Observer*, XXXVIII (December, 1914), 9–10.

"Wild Game," *Nation*, CXXII (June 2, 1926), 605. *The Long Street*, p. 75.

"Woodlands, 1956–60," *The Long Street*, pp. 25–27.

"X, Y and Z," *Archive* (April, 1926), 22. R. P. Harriss, ed., *The Archive Anthology* (Durham: Duke University Press, 1926), p. 24.

IV. *Essays and Articles*

"A Mirror for Artists," Twelve Southerners, *I'll Take My Stand, The South and the Agrarian Tradition* (New York: Harper and Brothers Publishers, 1930), pp. 28–60. Reissued: Introduction by Louis D. Rubin, Jr., Biographical Sketches by Virginia Rock, Harper Torchbooks, The Academy Library (New York: Harper and Brothers, 1962).

"A Note on American Heroes," *Southern Review*, I (December, 1935), 436–448. *The Attack on Leviathan*, pp. 212–227.

"An Agrarian Looks at the New Deal," *Free America*, II (June, 1938), 3–5, 17.

"Agrarianism and Politics," *Review of Politics*, I (April, 1939), 114–125.

"American Heroes," see "A Note on American Heroes."

"Analysis of Elizabeth Madox Roberts' *A Buried Treasure*," *Creative Reading*, VI (December 1, 1931), 1235–1249.

"Analysis of John Cowper Powys's *Wolf Solent*," *Creative Reading*, III (August 1, 1929), 9–25.

"Analysis of Katherine Brush's *Young Man of Manhattan*," *Creative Reading*, IV (January 15, 1930), 81–95.

"Analysis of Louis Bromfield's *The Strange Case of Miss Annie Spragg*," *Creative Reading*, III (February 15, 1929), 9–25.

"Analysis of Ludwig Lewisohn's *The Last Days of Shylock*," *Creative Reading*, V (February 15, 1931), 870–886.

"Analysis of Maristan Chapman's *The Happy Mountain*," *Creative Reading*, II (September 15, 1928), 9–24.

"Artist as Southerner," *Saturday Review of Literature*, II (May 15, 1926), 781–783. St. Petersburg *Times*, June 6, 1926.

"Certain Fallacies in Modern Poetry," *Fugitive*, III (June, 1924), 66–68.

"Counterattack, 1930–1940, The South Against Leviathan," *Southern Writers in the Modern World*, pp. 31–62.

"Criticism Outside New York," *Bookman*, LXXIII (May, 1931), 247–256. *The Spyglass*, pp. 239–256.

"Current Attitudes Toward Folklore," *Bulletin of the Tennessee Folklore Society*, VI (December, 1940), 44–51. *Still Rebels, Still Yankees*, pp. 128–136.

"Decorum in the Novel," *Modern Age*, IX (Winter, 1964–65), 34–48.

"Dilemma of the Southern Liberals," *American Mercury*, XXXI (February, 1934), 227–235. *The Attack on Leviathan*, pp. 261–284.

"Discussion of Emil Ludwig's *The Son of Man*," *Creative Reading*, II (September, 1928), 25–30.

"Discussion of George Fort Milton's *The Age of Hate*," *Creative Reading*, V (February 15, 1931), 887–892.

"Discussion of Herbert Asbury's *Carry Nation*," *Creative Reading*, III (November 1, 1929), 25–30.

"Discussion of James Truslow Adams' *Epic of America*," *Creative Reading*, VI (December 1, 1931), 1250–1256.

"Discussion of Lola Ridge's *Firehead*," *Creative Reading*, IV (January 15, 1930), 96–102.

"Discussion of René Fulop-Miller's *Rasputin: The Holy Devil*," *Creative Reading*, III (February 15, 1929), 26–30.

"Donald Davidson, Southern Writer, Sees Rot in 'Yale Review' Diagnosis of South's Progress," *Yale Daily News*, LIV (March 30, 1931), 1, 5. [A reply to Clarence E. Cason, "Is the South Advancing?", *Yale Review*, XX (March, 1931), 502–514.] Clarksville *Star*, April 17, 1931.

"Essays on Conrad's 'Suspense,' IV," *Saturday Review of Literature*, II (November 21, 1925), 315, 326. [Fourth Prize essay in contest for best suggested endings to Conrad's unfinished novel "Suspense."]

"Expedients versus Principles—Cross-Purposes in the South,"

Southern Review, II (April, 1937), 647–669. *The Attack on Leviathan,* pp. 312–338.

"Faulkner e Warren a contribuição do Sul dos Estados Unidos para a literatura norte-americana contemporânea," *Anhembi* (São Paulo), I (Dezembro, 1950), 34–43. [Translated into Portuguese.]

"Federation or Disunion," see "That This Nation May Endure."

"First Fruits of Dayton, The Intellectual Evolution in Dixie," *Forum,* LXXIX (June, 1928), 896–907. [Discussion: W. P. Hobby, "Southern Progress," *Forum,* LXXX (August, 1928), 312–313.]

"Foreword," Jesse Hill Ford, *The Conversion of Buster Drumwright* (Nashville: Vanderbilt University Press, 1964), pp. xv–xxiv.

"Futurism and Archaism in Toynbee and Hardy," *Still Rebels, Still Yankees,* pp. 62–83.

"Grammar and Rhetoric: The Teacher's Problem," *Quarterly Journal of Speech,* XXXIX (December, 1953), 425–436.

"Howard Odum and the Sociological Proteus," see Periodical Book Reviews, Odum, Howard, *Southern Regions of the United States.*

"I'll Take My Stand: A History," *American Review,* V (Summer, 1935), 301–321.

"In Justice to So Fine a Country," see Periodical Book Reviews, Hubbell, Jay B., *The South in American Literature.*

"In Memory of John Gould Fletcher," *Poetry,* LXXVII (December, 1950), 154–161. *Still Rebels, Still Yankees,* pp. 31–40.

"Introduction," Rollin Lasseter, *Flags and Other Poems* (Nashville: Robert Moore Allen, 1963), [pages unnumbered].

"Introduction," Mary C. Simms Oliphant, Alfred Taylor Odell, and T. C. Duncan Eaves, eds., *The Letters of William Gilmore Simms,* vol. I (Columbia: University of South Carolina Press, 1952), pp. xxxi–lviii.

"Introduction," Stark Young, *So Red the Rose,* Modern Standard Authors Edition (New York: Charles Scribner's Sons, 1953), pp. v–xxxvi. Condensed as "Theme and Method in *So Red the Rose,*" *Hopkins Review,* VI (Spring-Summer, 1953), 85–100. Louis D. Rubin, Jr., and Robert D. Jacobs, eds., *Southern Renascence* (Baltimore: Johns Hopkins Press, 1953), pp. 262–277. *Still Rebels, Still Yankees,* pp. 84–101.

"Joseph Conrad's Directed Indirections," *Sewanee Review* XXXIII (April, 1925), 163–177.

"Le Sudiste," *Esprit* (Paris), No. 127 (November, 1946), 582–591. ["L'Homme Americain" issue. Translated into French.]

"Making a Livelihood on the Farm, An Agrarian Answers Some Criticisms," Richmond *Times Dispatch,* February 15, 1931, Section II, p. 2.

"Malone, Walter," Dumas Malone, ed., *Dictionary of American Biography,* vol. XII (New York: Charles Scribner's Sons, 1933), p. 227.

"Marling, John Leake," Dumas Malone, ed., *Dictionary of American Biography,* vol. XII (New York: Charles Scribner's Sons, 1933), pp. 289–290.

"Meeting of Southern Writers," *Bookman,* LXXIV (January and February, 1934), 132–133.

"Moore, John Trotwood," Dumas Malone, ed. *Dictionary of American Biography,* vol. XIII (New York: Charles Scribner's Sons, 1934), pp. 132–133. Henry W. Wells, *Poet and Psychiatrist Merrill Moore, M. D.* (New York: Twayne Publishers, 1955), pp. 20–21 [partially reprinted].

"Mr. Babbitt at Philadelphia," *Southern Review,* VI (Spring, 1941), 695–703.

"Mr. Cash and the Proto-Dorian South," see Periodical Book Reviews, Cash, W. J., *The Mind of the South.*

"New York and the Hinterland," *American Review,* III (October, 1934), 545–561. *The Attack on Leviathan,* pp. 155–168. *Still Rebels, Still Yankees,* pp. 254–266.

"On Being in Hock to the North," *Free America,* III (May, 1939), 3–6.

"Poetry As Tradition," *Still Rebels, Still Yankees,* pp. 3–22.

"Political Regionalism and Administrative Regionalism," *Annals of the American Academy of Political and Social Science,* CCVII (January, 1940), 138-143.

"Preface," Wilbur Foster Creighton, *Yo, A Yarn of the Spanish Main* (Nashville: Privately Published, 1930).

"Preface," *Vermont Chap Book, Being a Garland of Ten Folk*

Ballads (Middlebury, Vermont: Hand Set by the Bread Loaf Printers for the Middlebury College Press, 1941), pp. v–viii.

"Preface to Decision," *Sewanee Review,* LIII (Summer, 1945), 394–412.

"Pullin' Corn: A New Georgia Scene," Vanderbilt *Vagabond,* III (March, 1959), 20–22.

"Recollections of Robert Frost," *Robert Frost and Bread Loaf,* A Limited Edition (Middlebury, Vermont: The Middlebury College Press, 1964), [pages unnumbered].

"Regionalism," William T. Couch, ed., *Collier's 1954 Year Book* (New York: P. F. Collier's and Son, 1954), pp. 506–509.

"Regionalism and Education," *American Review,* IV (January, 1935), 310–325. *The Attack on Leviathan,* pp. 240–257.

"Regionalism and Nationalism in American Literature," *American Review,* V (April, 1935), 48–61. *The Attack on Leviathan,* pp. 228–239. *Still Rebels, Still Yankees,* pp. 267–278.

"Regionalism as Social Science," *Southern Review,* III (October, 1937), 209–224. *The Attack on Leviathan,* pp. 39–64.

"Regionalism in the Arts," *Attack on Leviathan,* pp. 65–101. [Incorporates portions of "Sectionalism in the United States."]

"Richmond Croom Beatty: A Memoir," William E. Walker and Robert L. Welker, eds., *Reality and Myth, Essays in American Literature in Memory of Richmond Croom Beatty* (Nashville: Vanderbilt University Press, 1964), pp. 3–14.

"Sectionalism in the United States," *Hound and Horn,* VI (July–September, 1933), 561–589. [See "Regionalism in the Arts," "The Diversity of America," and "Two Interpretations of American History."]

"Social Science Discovers Regionalism," see "Regionalism as Social Science."

"Some Day in Old Charleston," *Georgia Review,* III (Summer, 1949), 150–161. *Still Rebels, Still Yankees,* pp. 213–227.

" 'Southern Agrarians' State Their Case," *Progressive Farmer,* LI (June, 1936), 5, 26.

"Southern Literature—1931," *Creative Reading,* VI (December 1, 1931), 1229–1234.

"Still Rebels, Still Yankees," *American Review,* II (November, 1933), 58–72; (December, 1933), 175–188. *The Attack on*

Leviathan, pp. 131–154. Irving H. White, George B. Franklin, and Edward A. Post, eds., *Essays in Value* (New York: D. Appleton–Century, 1938), pp. 131–150. Donald Davidson, *American Composition and Rhetoric* (New York: Charles Scribner's Sons, 1939), pp. 111–120; Revised Edition in Collaboration with Ivar Lou Myhr (1947), pp. 87–94; Third Edition (1953), pp. 89–97 [partially reprinted under the title "Brother Jonathan and Cousin Roderick"]. Richmond Croom Beatty and William Perry Fidler, eds. *Contemporary Southern Prose* (Boston: D. C. Heath and Company, 1940), pp. 5–24. Richmond Croom Beatty, ed., *A Vanderbilt Miscellany 1919–1944* (Nashville: Vanderbilt University Press, 1944), pp. 157–178. Howard Mumford Jones, Richard M. Ludwig, and Marvin B. Perry, eds., *Modern Minds, An Anthology of Ideas* (Boston: D. C. Heath and Company, 1949), pp. 77–93. Richmond Croom Beatty, Floyd C. Watkins, and Thomas Daniel Young, eds., *The Literature of the South* (Chicago: Scott, Foresman and Company, 1952), pp. 772–784. *Still Rebels, Still Yankees*, pp. 231–253.

"That This Nation May Endure, The Need for Political Regionalism," Herbert Agar and Allen Tate, eds., *Who Owns America? A New Declaration of Independence* (Boston: Houghton Mifflin Company, 1936), pp. 113–134. *The Attack on Leviathan*, pp. 102–128 [as "Federation or Disunion: The Political Economy of Regionalism"]. A. Theodore Johnson and Allen Tate, eds., *America Through the Essay* (Oxford: Oxford University Press, 1938), pp. 149–171.

"The Anti-Scientific Mind," *Creative Reading*, III (August 1, 1929), 3–8.

"The City Mind in Literature," *Creative Reading*, IV (January 15, 1930), 75–80.

"The Class Approach to Southern Problems," *Southern Review*, V (Autumn, 1939), 261–272.

"The Diversity of America," *The Attack on Leviathan*, pp. 3–12. [Incorporates portions of "Sectionalism in the United States."]

"The English Teacher and the Lost Humanities," *Harvard Graduates' Magazine*, XLII (March, 1934), 177–188.

"The Forty-three Best Southern Novels for Readers and Collectors," *Publishers Weekly*, CXXVII (April 27, 1935), 1675–1676.

"The Great Plains," *The Attack on Leviathan*, pp. 192–211.

"The Lady or the Tiger," *The Vanderbilt Observer*, XXXII (January, 1910), 128–129.

"The Local Color Novel," *Creative Reading*, II (September 15, 1928), 3–8.

"The 'Mystery' of the Agrarians: Facts and Illusions About Some Southern Writers," *Saturday Review of Literature*, XXVI (January 23, 1943), 6–7.

"The New South and the Conservative Tradition," *National Review*, IX (September 10, 1960), 141–146.

"The Novel as Story," *Creative Reading*, III (February 15, 1929), 3–8.

"The Origins of Our Heroes," see Periodical Book Reviews, Wecter, Dixon, *The Hero in America*.

"The Political Economy of Regionalism," *American Review*, VI (February, 1936), 410–434.

"The Reality of the Unreal," *The Vanderbilt Observer*, XXXVII (June, 1915), 28–32.

"The Sacred Harp in the Land of Eden," *Virginia Quarterly Review*, X (April, 1934), 203–217. *Reader's Digest*, XXIV (May, 1934), 83–86 [condensed under title "Songs of the Sacred Harp"]. *Still Rebels, Still Yankees*, pp. 137–151.

"The Shape of Things and Men," *American Review*, VII (Summer, 1936), 225–248. *The Attack on Leviathan*, pp. 349–368.

"The South Today: Report on Southern Literature," Dallas *Times Herald*, July 17, 1938, Section I, p. 6.

"The Southern Poet and His Tradition," *Poetry*, XL (May, 1932), 94–103. Edd Winfield Parks, ed., *Southern Poets* (New York: American Book Company, 1936), pp. 369–375. *The Attack on Leviathan*, pp. 339–346.

"The Southern Writer and the Modern University," *Georgia Review*, XII (Spring, 1958), 18–28. *Southern Writers in the Modern World*, pp. 63–76.

"The Talking Oaks of the South," *Shenandoah*, V (Winter, 1953), 3–8.

"The Thankless Muse and Her Fugitive Poets," *Sewanee Review*, LXVI (Spring, 1958), 201–228. *Southern Writers in the Modern World*, pp. 1–30.

"The Tradition of Irreverence," *Still Rebels, Still Yankees*, pp. 105–127.

"The Traditional Basis of Thomas Hardy's Fiction," *Southern Review*, VI (Summer, 1940), 162–178. *Still Rebels, Still Yankees*, pp. 43–61. Albert J. Guerard, ed., *Hardy, A Collection of Critical Essays*, Twentieth Century Views (Englewood Cliffs, New Jersey: Prentice Hall, 1963), pp. 10–23.

"The Trend of Literature, A Partisan View," W. T. Couch, ed., *Culture in the South* (Chapel Hill: The University of North Carolina Press, 1935), pp. 183–210.

"The Two Old Wests," *American Review*, IV (November, 1934), 29–55. *The Attack on Leviathan*, pp. 169–191.

"The Unhappy Role of Science, 1956," *V Square, the Vanderbilt Engineering Magazine*, VII (January, 1956), 6, 22.

"The Vanderbilt Literary Tradition," Preface to *Pursuit Anthology of Stories and Poems* (Nashville: The Calumet Club of Vanderbilt University, 1951), pp. 9–13. *Vanderbilt Alumnus*, XLI (May-June, 1956), 7–8.

"The White Spirituals and Their Historian," *Sewanee Review*, LI (Autumn, 1943), 589–598.

"Theme and Method in *So Red the Rose*," see "Introduction," Stark Young, *So Red the Rose*.

"3,500 Pack Hall as Ransom, Barr Debate Southern Problems," Chattanooga *News*, November 15, 1930, p. 11. [Brief news report on debate between Stringfellow Barr and John Crowe Ransom at Richmond, Virginia.]

"Two Interpretations of American History," *The Attack on Leviathan*, pp. 13–38. [Incorporates portions of "Sectionalism in the United States."]

"What Does History Mean?", *Creative Reading*, V (February 15, 1931), 865–869.

"Where Regionalism and Sectionalism Meet," *Social Forces*, XIII (October, 1934), 23–31.

"White Spirituals: The Choral Music of the South," *American Scholar*, IV (Autumn, 1935), 460–473.

"Whither Dixie?—Mr. Barr and Mr. Ransom in the Great Debate at Richmond," Chattanooga *News*, November 22, 1930, p. 25. [Full news report on the debate between Stringfellow Barr and John Crowe Ransom at Richmond, Virginia.]

"Why the Modern South Has a Great Literature," Richmond C. Beatty, J. Philip Hyatt, and Monroe K. Spears, eds., *Vanderbilt Studies in the Humanities*, vol. I (Nashville: Vanderbilt University Press, 1951), pp. 1–17. *Still Rebels, Still Yankees*, pp. 159–179.

"Yeats and the Centaur," *Southern Review*, VII (Winter, 1941), 510–516. James Hall and Martin Steinman, eds., *The Permanence of Yeats* (New York: The Macmillan Company, 1950), pp. 278–285. *Still Rebels, Still Yankees*, pp. 23–30.

V. Periodical Book Reviews

Æ. *Vale and Other Poems, Virginia Quarterly Review,* VII (July, 1931), 432–440.

ALLEN, HERVEY. *Earth Moods, Fugitive,* IV (September, 1925), 94–95.

ANDERSON, SHERWOOD. *Puzzled America, American Review,* V (May, 1935), 234–238.

ARNOW, HARRIETTE. *Seedtime on the Cumberland,* New York *Herald Tribune Book Review,* September 4, 1960, pp. 1, 12.

AUDEN, W. H., and CHRISTOPHER ISHERWOOD. *The Day Beneath the Skin, Southern Review,* I (April, 1936), 875–887.

BAKER, O. E., RALPH BORSODI, and M. L. WILSON. *Agriculture in Modern Life, Free America,* III (December, 1939), 18–19.

BECK, HORACE P. *The Folklore of Maine, The Middlebury College News Letter,* XXXII (Autumn, 1957), 28.

BLAKE, HOWARD. *Prolegomena to Any Future Poetry, Southern Review,* I (April, 1936), 875–887.

BOATRIGHT, MODY C., WILSON M. HUDSON, and ALLEN MAXWELL, eds. *Texas Folk and Folklore, Journal of American Folklore,* LXIX (January-March, 1956), 85–86.

BORSODI, RALPH. *This Ugly Civilization, American Review* I (May, 1939), 238–242.

BOTKIN, B. A., ed. *A Treasury of American Folklore, Western Folklore,* IX (July, 1950), 283–285.

BROWNELL, BAKER. *The Philosopher in Chaos, Free America,* V (July, 1941), 17–18.

CALDWELL, ERSKINE, and MARGARET BOURKE-WHITE. *You Have Seen Their Faces, Southern Review,* IV (July, 1938), 15–25.

Richmond Croom Beatty, and William Perry Fidler, eds. *Contemporary Southern Prose* (Boston: D. C. Heath and Company, 1940), pp. 267–277.

Calverton, V. F. *The Awakening of America, Free America* IV (February, 1940), 19–20.

Campbell, Roy. *Adamastor, Virginia Quarterly Review,* VII (July, 1931), 432–440.

Cash, W. J. *The Mind of the South, Southern Review,* VII (Summer, 1941), 1–20. *Still Rebels, Still Yankees,* pp. 191–212.

Cauley, Troy J. *Agrarianism: A Program for Farmers, American Review,* V (April, 1935), 106–112.

Cheney, Brainard. *River Rogue, Sewanee Review,* LI (Winter, 1943), 163–169.

Clay, Cassius M. *The Mainstay of American Individualism, American Review,* III (April, 1934), 96–101.

Coyle, David Cushman. *Roads to a New America, Free America,* III (February, 1939), 19–20.

Cummings, E. E. *XLI Poems, Fugitive,* IV (September, 1925), 94–95.

Dabney, Virginius. *Liberalism in the South, Saturday Review of Literature,* IX (February 11, 1933), 423.

Denney, Reuel. *The Astonished Muse, National Review,* IV (October 12, 1957), 333–334.

Deutsch, Babette. *Epistle to Prometheus, Virginia Quarterly Review,* VII (July, 1931), 432–440.

Dollard, John. *Caste and Class in a Southern Town, American Review,* IX (May, 1937), 152–172.

Dowdey, Clifford. *The Seven Days: The Emergence of Lee, Modern Age,* IX (Winter, 1964–65), 109–111.

Dunsany, Lord. *The King of Elfland's Daughter, The Guardian,* I (February, 1925), 146–147.

Eliot, T. S. *Ash Wednesday, Virginia Quarterly Review,* VII (July, 1931), 432–440.

———. *Homage to John Dryden, Fugitive,* IV (June, 1925), 61–62.

Ernst, Morris L. *Too Big, Free America,* IV (August, 1940), 18–19.

FITTS, DUDLEY, and ROBERT FITZGERALD. *Sophocles: Oedipus Rex, An English Version, Shenandoah,* I (Summer, 1950), 39–44.

FITZGERALD, ROBERT. *Poems, Southern Review,* I (April, 1936), 875–887.

FRANK, WALDO. *Life and Death of David Markand, American Review,* IV (December, 1934), 233–238.

GILBERT, RUDOLPH. *Shine Perishing Republic: Robinson Jeffers and the Tragic Sense in Modern Poetry, American Literature,* IX (May, 1937), 273–274.

HARRIS, EVELYN. *The Barter Lady, American Review,* III (September, 1934), 526–530.

HUBBELL, JAY B. *The South in American Literature, 1607–1900, Sewanee Review,* LXIII (Winter, 1955), 144–152. *Still Rebels, Still Yankees,* pp. 180–190.

HUDSON, ARTHUR PALMER. *Humor of the Old Deep South, American Review,* VII (Summer, 1936), 335–341.

JEFFERS, ROBINSON. *Solstice and Other Poems, Southern Review,* I (April, 1936), 875–887.

JENSEN, MERRILL, ed. *Regionalism in America, American Literature,* XXIV (March, 1952), 93–96.

KANTOR, MACKINLAY. *Andersonville, National Review,* I (May 9, 1956), 20–21.

KORNGOLD, RALPH. *Thaddeus Stevens: A Being Darkly Wise and Rudely Great, National Review,* I (December 7, 1955), 28–29.

LA FARGE, CHRISTOPHER. *Hoxsie Sells His Acres, American Review,* III (June, 1934), 402–407.

LOVEMAN, SAMUEL. *The Hermaphrodite and Other Poems, Southern Review,* I (April, 1936), 875–887.

MACLEISH, ARCHIBALD. *The Pot of Earth, Fugitive,* IV (June, 1925), 62–63.

MILLAY, EDNA ST. VINCENT. *Fatal Interview, Virginia Quarterly Review,* VII (July, 1931), 432–440.

MILLER, HENRY PICKENS. *The Blessings of Liberty, American Review,* IX (October, 1937), 456–481.

MUMFORD, LEWIS. *Faith for Living, Free America,* IV (October, 1940), 19.

NATHAN, ROBERT. *Selected Poems, Southern Review,* I (April, 1936), 875–887.

O'CONNOR, FLANNERY. *The Violent Bear it Away,* New York *Times Book Review,* February 28, 1960, p. 4.

ODUM, HOWARD. *Southern Regions of the United States, American Review,* VIII (February, 1937), 385–417. *The Attack on Leviathan,* pp. 285–311.

———, and HARRY ESTILL MOORE. *American Regionalism, Free America,* II (October, 1938), 19–20.

PARKS, EDD WINFIELD. *Segments of Southern Thought,* Nashville *Banner,* March 15, 1939, Section X, p. 4.

———. *William Gilmore Simms as Literary Critic, South Atlantic Quarterly,* LXI (Winter, 1962), 111.

RANSOM, JOHN CROWE. *Grace After Meat, The Guardian,* II (October, 1925), 456–458.

RAPER, ARTHUR F. *Preface to Peasantry: A Tale of Two Black Belt Countries, American Review,* VIII (December, 1936), 177–204.

ROUSE, BLAIR, ed. *Letters of Ellen Glasgow,* New York *Times Book Review,* January 19, 1958, pp. 7, 14.

SCHLESINGER, ARTHUR MEIER. *The Rise of the City, American Review,* I (April, 1933), 100–104.

TATE, ALLEN. *Stonewall Jackson: The Good Soldier* (Reprint), *Modern Age,* II (Fall, 1958), 416–419.

TREVELYAN, R. C. *Thamyris, Fugitive,* IV (December, 1925), 126–128.

VAN DOREN, MARK. *Jonathan Gentry, Virginia Quarterly* VII (July, 1931), 432–440.

WARNER, SYLVIA TOWNSEND. *Opus 7, Virginia Quarterly Review,* VII (July, 1931), 432–440.

WECTER, DIXON. *The Hero in America: A Chronicle of Hero-Worship, Kenyon Review,* III (Autumn, 1941), 510–514. Donald Davidson, *American Composition and Rhetoric,* Third Edition (New York: Charles Scribner's Sons, 1953), pp. 484–487. *Still Rebels, Still Yankees,* pp. 152–156.

WHALER, JAMES. *A Poem for Rafinesque, Virginia Quarterly Review,* VII (July, 1931), 432–440.

WHITE, NEWMAN IVEY, PAULL F. BAUM, *et al.,* eds. *The Frank C. Brown Collection of North Carolina Folklore,* vols. I, II, and III, *Journal of Southern History,* IX (February, 1953), 114–116.

WILSON, CHARLES MORROW. *Backwoods America, American Review,* IV (March, 1935), 622–627.

VI. Nashville Tennessean Book Page Reviews

ADAMS, JAMES TRUSLOW. *Our Business Civilization,* December 1, 1929. *The Spyglass,* pp. 229–233.

ADAMS, SAMUEL HOPKINS. *Revelry,* February 13, 1927.

———. *Siege,* March 2, 1924.

ADÈS, ALBERT. *A Naked King,* February 8, 1925.

AIKEN, CONRAD. *Blue Voyage,* August 14, 1927.

———. *Priapus and the Pool,* January 3, 1926.

———, ed. *American Poetry,* April 3, 1927.

ALLEN, HERVEY. *Earth Moods,* July 19, 1925.

———. *Toward the Flame,* May 2, 1926.

American Poetry, 1925: A Miscellany, September 30, 1925.

American Poetry, 1927: A Miscellany, October 16, 1927.

ANDERSON, MAXWELL, and LAURENCE STALLINGS. *Three American Plays,* October 31, 1926.

ANDERSON, SHERWOOD. *A New Testament,* July 3, 1927.

———. *A Story Teller's Story,* January 18, 1925.

———. *Dark Laughter,* October 11, 1925.

———. *Sherwood Anderson's Notebook,* June 6, 1926.

ANTHONY, JOSEPH, ed. *The Best News Stories of 1923,* August 24, 1924.

ARMSTRONG, ANNE W. *This Day and Time,* September 7, 1930.

ATHERTON, GERTRUDE. *The Crystal Cup,* September 6, 1925.

AUSLANDER, JOSEPH. *Cyclops' Eye,* May 30, 1926.

———. *Sunrise Trumpets,* June 22, 1924.

BAILEY, H. C. *The Merchant Prince,* December 22, 1929.

BAILEY, JOHN. *Walt Whitman,* July 11, 1926.

BATES, ERNEST SUTHERLAND. *This Land of Liberty,* August 25, 1930.

BEALE, HOWARD K. *The Critical Year, A Study of Andrew Johnson and Reconstruction,* June 29, 1930.

BEARD, CHARLES A. and MARY. *The Rise of American Civilization,* March 2, 1930.

BECKE, LOUIS. *Edward Barry,* April 13, 1924.

BEEBE, WILLIAM. *Beneath Tropic Seas,* October 21, 1928.

———. *The Arcturus Adventure,* June 20, 1926.

BEER, THOMAS. *Sandoval,* July 6, 1924.

———. *The Mauve Decade,* June 27, 1926.

BENEFIELD, BARRY. *The Chicken-Wagon Family,* September 12, 1926.

BENNETT, ARNOLD. *Lord Raingo,* December 26, 1926.

BENT, SILAS. *Ballyhoo,* November 6, 1927.

———. *Machine Made Man,* May 4, 1930.

BEST, AGNES. *Thomas Paine,* July 10, 1927.

BIBESCO, MARTHE. *Catherine-Paris,* June 3, 1928.

BLACKWOOD, ALGERNON. *Tongues of Fire,* April 5, 1925.

BLUNDEN, EDMUND. *Undertones of War,* June 16, 1929.

BODENHEIM, MAXWELL. *Returning to Emotion,* July 3, 1927.

BORSODI, RALPH. *This Ugly Civilization,* December 1, 1929. *The Spyglass,* pp. 229–233.

BOWERS, CLAUDE G. *The Tragic Era,* September 15, 1929. *The Spyglass,* pp. 217–224.

BOYD, JAMES. *Drums,* August 2, 1925.

———. *Long Hunt,* April 27, 1930.

———. *Marching On,* May 15, 1927.

BOYD, THOMAS. *Points of Honor,* March 29, 1925.

———. *Shadow of the Long Knives,* July 1, 1928.

BRADFORD, GAMALIEL. *The Soul of Samuel Pepys,* June 1, 1924.

BRADFORD, ROARK. *Ol' King David an' the Philistine Boys,* April 20, 1930. *The Spyglass,* pp. 53–55.

———. *This Side of Jordan,* February 17, 1929.

BROMFIELD, LOUIS. *The Strange Case of Miss Annie Spragg,* September 23, 1928. *The Spyglass,* pp. 83–87.

BROOKS, VAN WYCK. *Emerson and Others*, May 22, 1927.

————, ed. *The American Caravan*, October 9, 1927.

BROWN, OSWALD EUGENE, JAMES HAMPTON KIRKLAND, and EDWIN MIMS. *God and the New Knowledge* (Cole Lectures, Vanderbilt University), August 8, 1926.

BUCHAN, JOHN. *Salute to Adventurers*, April 20, 1930.

BYNNER, WITTER. *Caravan*, October 25, 1925.

BYRNE, DONN. *Blind Raftery*, November 2, 1924.

CABELL, JAMES BRANCH. *Something About Eve*, October 23, 1927.

————. *The Way of Ecben*, February 16, 1930. *The Spyglass*, pp. 40–44.

CANBY, HENRY SEIDEL. *American Estimates*, June 23, 1929. *The Spyglass*, pp. 137–142.

CATHER, WILLA. *Death Comes for the Archbishop*, September 25, 1927.

————. *My Ántonia*, September 19, 1926.

————. *My Mortal Enemy*, November 14, 1926.

CHAPMAN, MARISTAN. *The Happy Mountain*, August 19, 1928.

CHARTERIS, JOHN. *Field-Marshall Earl Haig*, May 5, 1929.

CHASE, STUART. *Prosperity: Fact or Myth*, January 26, 1930.

CHESTERTON, GILBERT K. *St. Francis of Assisi*, March 9, 1924.

————,et al. *Number Two Jay Street*, November 9, 1924.

CLARK, EMILY. *Stuffed Peacocks*, October 9, 1927.

CLIFFORD, SIR HUGH. *The Further Side of Silence*, November 13, 1927.

COBB, IRVIN S. *Cobb's American Guyed Books*, April 27, 1924.

CODY, SHERWIN. *Poe: Man, Poet and Creative Thinker*, June 29, 1924.

CONANT, ISABEL FISKE. *Many Wings*, April 6, 1924.

CONKLING, GRACE HAZARD. *Sonnets or a Dark Lover*, October 17, 1926.

CONRAD, JOSEPH. *Tales of Hearsay*, February 15, 1925.

————. *The Rover*, February 10, 1924.

CRANE, HART. *White Buildings*, April 3, 1927. *The Spyglass*, pp. 106–109.

CROSS, RUTH. *The Golden Cocoon*, May 18, 1924.

CUMMINGS, E. E. *XLI Poems*, June 21, 1925.

CURRY, WALTER CLYDE. *Chaucer and the Medieval Sciences,* December 5, 1926.

DAMON, S. FOSTER. *Thomas Holly Chivers,* June 1, 1930.

DAMROSCH, WALTER. *My Musical Life,* September 19, 1926.

DANTZIG, TOBIAS. *Number, the Language of Science,* September 14, 1930.

DARGAN, OLIVE TILFORD. *Highland Annals,* March 14, 1926.

DAVIESS, MARIA THOMPSON. *Seven Times Seven,* May 11, 1924.

DAVIS, WILLIAM STEARNS. *The Whirlwind,* December 22, 1929.

DENNIS, GEOFFREY. *Harvest in Poland,* April 26, 1925.

DEVAL, JACQUES. *Wooden Swords,* July 27, 1930.

DESTI, MARY. *The Untold Story,* February 24, 1929.

DICKMAN, JOSEPH T. *The Great Crusade,* March 20, 1927.

DODGE, DANIEL KILLIAM. *Abraham Lincoln, Master of Words,* September 28, 1924.

DOS PASSOS, JOHN. *Manhattan Transfer,* May 16, 1926.

DOUGLAS, NORMAN. *Goodbye to Western Culture,* September 21, 1930.

DREISER, THEODORE. *An American Tragedy,* January 31, 1926. *The Spyglass,* pp. 67–70.

DU BOIS, W. E. B. *Dark Princess,* July 1, 1928.

DUFFUS, R. L. *Books: Their Place in a Democracy,* August 3, 1930. *The Spyglass,* pp. 184–188.

DURANT, WILL. *The Story of Philosophy,* September 26, 1926.

EARLE, ALICE MORSE. *Colonial Dames and Good Wives,* August 17, 1924.

EDDISON, E. R. *Styrbiorn the Strong,* October 10, 1926.

———. *The Worm Ouroboros,* August 22, 1926.

ELIOT, T. S. *For Lancelot Andrewes,* June 23, 1929. *The Spyglass,* pp. 137–142.

ENCYCLOPAEDIA BRITANNICA. *These Eventful Years: The Twentieth Century in the Making,* September 21, 1924.

FARRAR, JOHN. *The Middle Twenties,* August 3, 1924.

FARRELL, ANDREW. *John Cameron's Odyssey,* November 25, 1928.

FAULKNER, WILLIAM. *Mosquitoes,* July 3, 1927.

———. *Sartoris,* April 14, 1929.

———. *Soldiers' Pay,* April 11, 1926.

FERBER, EDNA. *Showboat,* August 22, 1926. *The Spyglass,* pp. 70–74.

FIGGIS, DARRELL. *The Return of the Hero,* June 29, 1930.

FINGER, CHARLES J. *Frontier Ballads,* October 16, 1927.

FLEMING, WALTER L. *The Freedmen's Savings Bank,* December 18, 1927.

FLETCHER, JOHN GOULD. *Branches of Adam,* September 25, 1927.

———. *The Black Rock,* December 2, 1928.

———. *The Two Frontiers,* May 25, 1930.

FOERSTER, NORMAN, ed. *Humanism and America,* March 9, 1930.

FORD, FORD MADOX. *Joseph Conrad: A Personal Remembrance,* January 25, 1925.

FORD, HENRY, and SAMUEL CROWTHER. *Moving Forward,* November 9, 1930. *The Spyglass,* pp. 234–238.

FORT, JOHN P. *Light in the Window,* June 10, 1928.

———. *Stone Daugherty,* May 12, 1929.

FREDENBURGH, THEODORE. *Soldiers March!,* October 5, 1930.

FROST, ROBERT. *Selected Poems,* December 30, 1928.

———. *West-Running Brook,* December 30, 1928.

GALE, ZONA. *Preface to a Life,* February 6, 1927. *The Spyglass,* pp. 153–158.

GARNETT, DAVID. *Go She Must!,* March 6, 1927.

GIBBS, A. HAMILTON. *Gun Fodder,* April 13, 1924.

GLASGOW, ELLEN. *The Old Dominion Edition of the Works of Ellen Glasgow,* April 13, 1930. *The Spyglass,* pp. 49–53.

———. *The Romantic Comedians,* October 10, 1926.

GOLDBERG, ISAAC. *The Theatre of George Jean Nathan,* January 9, 1927.

GOURMONT, RÉMY DE. *A Night in the Luxembourg,* September 12, 1926.

GRAVES, ROBERT. *Good-Bye to All That,* February 2, 1930.

———. *Lawrence and the Arabian Adventure,* June 17, 1928.

GRAY, JOHN CHIPMAN. *War Letters of John Chipman Gray and John Codman Ropes, 1862–1865,* February 19, 1928.

GREEN, JULIAN. *The Dark Journey,* December 8, 1929. *The Spyglass,* pp. 93–95.

GREEN, PAUL. *The Field God and In Abraham's Bosom,* May 1, 1927.
———. *Wide Fields,* May 6, 1928.
GREENE, WILLIAM C., ed. *The Dialogues of Plato,* July 24, 1927.
GRIERSON, H. J. C., ed. *Poems of Lord Byron,* May 11, 1924.
GRISWOLD, FRANCIS. *The Tides of Malvern,* October 5, 1930.
HAINS, T. JENKINS. *The Black Barque,* April 20, 1924.
HALL, BERT, and JOHN J. NILES. *One Man's War,* May 9, 1929.
HANDY, W. C., ed. *Blues: An Anthology,* July 4, 1926.
HARDY, FLORENCE EMILY. *The Early Life of Thomas Hardy, 1840–1891,* March 10, 1929.
HARDY, THOMAS. *Human Shows, Far Phantasies, Songs and Trifles,* March 7, 1926. *The Spyglass,* pp. 102–104.
HASEK, JAROSLAV, *The Good Soldier: Schweik,* July 27, 1930.
HEMINGWAY, ERNEST. *A Farewell to Arms,* November 3, 1929. *The Spyglass,* pp. 88–92.
———. *Men Without Women,* January 22, 1928. *The Spyglass,* pp. 75–79.
HERGESHEIMER, JOSEPH. *Swords and Roses,* April 7, 1929.
HERVEY, HARRY. *King Cobra,* November 6, 1927.
HESSER, ETHELDA DAGGETT. *Inner Darkness,* July 13, 1924.
HEYWARD, DU BOSE. *Angel,* October 24, 1926.
———. *Mamba's Daughters,* February 3, 1929. *The Spyglass,* pp. 29–34.
———. *The Half Pint Flask,* September 22, 1929.
HILLYER, V. M. *A Child's History of the World,* November 9, 1929.
HODGSON, RALPH. *Poems,* January 11, 1925.
HOLLIS, CHRISTOPHER. *The American Heresy,* March 23, 1930.
HUDSON, A. P. *Specimens of Mississippi Folk-Lore,* December 9, 1928.
JAMES, MARQUIS. *The Raven, A Life Story of Sam Houston,* November 24, 1929.
JEFFERS, ROBINSON. *The Women at Point Sur,* August 7, 1929.
JOHNSON, CHARLES S. *The Negro in American Civilization,* July 20, 1930.
JOHNSON, GERALD W. *Andrew Jackson: An Epic in Homespun,* October 30, 1927.

———. *The Undefeated,* February 27, 1927.

JOHNSON, JAMES WELDON. *God's Trombones,* June 12, 1927.

———. *The Autobiography of an Ex-Colored Man,* September 11, 1927.

JOSEPHSON. MATHEW. *Portrait of the Artist as American,* June 22, 1930.

KELLERMANN, BERNHARD. *The Sea,* May 4, 1924.

KENNEDY, MARGARET. *The Constant Nymph,* March 8, 1925.

KENT, ROCKWELL. *Voyaging Southward From the Strait of Magellan,* October 26, 1924.

KEYNES, GEOFFREY, ed. *Works of William Blake,* Centenary Edition, March 11, 1928.

KEYSERLING, COUNT. *Europe,* July 8, 1928.

KIPLING, RUDYARD. *Debits and Credits,* October 10, 1926.

———. *Independence* (Rectorial Address), May 25, 1924.

KNICKERBOCKER, WILLIAM S., ed. *Classics of Modern Science,* July 24, 1927.

KOCH, FREDERICK H., ed. *Carolina Folk-Plays,* January 6, 1929.

KOMROFF, MANUEL, ed. *The Travels of Marco Polo,* March 21, 1926.

KREYMBORG, ALFRED. *Scarlet and Mellow,* May 30, 1926.

KROLL, HARRY HARRISON. *The Mountainy Singer,* September 16, 1928.

KRUTCH, JOSEPH WOOD. *Edgar Allan Poe: A Study in Genius,* April 4, 1926.

———. *The Modern Temper,* April 21, 1929.

LA SALE, ANTOINE DE. *The Fifteen Joys of Marriage,* April 17, 1927.

LAWRENCE, D. H. *Mornings in Mexico,* August 7, 1927.

———. *The Plumed Serpent,* March 1, 1926.

LAWRENCE, DAVID. *The True Story of Woodrow Wilson,* July 27, 1924.

LAWRENCE, T. E. *Revolt in the Desert,* April 10, 1927.

LAWSON, CHARLES. *You Can Change It,* February 24, 1924.

LESLIE, W. SEYMOUR. *The Silent Queen,* October 2, 1927.

LEWIS, SINCLAIR. *Arrowsmith,* March 15, 1925. *The Spyglass,* pp. 63–67.

————. *Dodsworth,* March 24, 1929.

————. *Elmer Gantry,* March 13, 1924.

————. *Mantrap,* June 6, 1926.

————. *The Man Who Knew Coolidge,* May 6, 1928.

LINDSAY, VACHEL. *Collected Poems,* January 3, 1926.

LOFTING, HUGH. *Doctor Doolittle's Circus,* November 9, 1924.

LOMAX, JOHN A. *Cowboy Songs and Other Frontier Ballads,* April 17, 1927.

LONDRES, ALBERT. *The Road to Buenos Ayres,* June 3, 1928.

LOWELL, AMY. *East Wind,* October 3, 1926.

————. *What's O'Clock,* September 13, 1925.

LOWES, JOHN LIVINGSTON. *The Road to Xanadu,* June 19, 1927. *The Spyglass,* pp. 131–137.

LUDOVICI, ANTHONY M. *Man: An Indictment,* June 12, 1927.

LULL, RICHARD SWANN. *The Ways of Life,* August 30, 1925.

MacGOWAN, KENNETH. *Footlights Across America,* January 19, 1930.

MacKENZIE, COMPTON. *The Parson's Progress,* February 24, 1924.

MacKENZIE, W. ROY. *Ballads and Sea-Songs from Nova Scotia,* May 27, 1928. *The Spyglass,* pp. 158–161.

MacLEISH, ARCHIBALD. *Streets in the Moon,* January 16, 1927.

————. *The Pot of Earth,* May 24, 1925.

M. M. *Memoirs of the Foreign Legion,* March 1, 1925.

MANN, THOMAS. *The Magic Mountain,* August 28, 1927.

MARKEY, MORRIS. *The Band Plays Dixie,* April 10, 1927.

MARKS, PERCY. *Martha,* March 22, 1925.

————. *The Plastic Age,* February 17, 1924.

MASEFIELD, JOHN. *Odtaa,* April 25, 1926.

————. *Sard Harker,* January 4, 1925.

————. *The Collected Works of John Masefield,* January 24, 1926. *The Spyglass,* pp. 99–102.

MASON, DANIEL GREGORY. *The Dilemma of American Music,* January 27, 1929. *The Spyglass,* pp. 170–175.

MASTERS, EDGAR LEE. *Jack Kelso: A Dramatic Poem,* September 2, 1928.

————. *Lee: A Dramatic Poem,* May 8, 1927.

MAURICE, FREDERICK, ed. *An Aide de Camp of Lee,* July 17, 1927.

———. *Robert E. Lee The Soldier,* May 3, 1925.

MAUROIS, ANDRE. *Ariel: The Life of Shelley,* June 29, 1924.

MEARNS, HUGHES. *Creative Power,* September 29, 1929.

MELLEN, GILMORE. *Sweet Man,* July 27, 1930.

MENCKEN, H. L. *Notes on Democracy,* December 12, 1926. *The Spyglass,* pp. 126–131.

MILFORD, H. S., ed. *The Oxford Book of Regency Verse,* March 17, 1929.

MILLAY, EDNA ST. VINCENT. *The Buck in the Snow,* December 2, 1928.

MIMS, EDWIN. *The Advancing South,* May 23, 1926.

MOLNAR, FRANZ. *Husbands and Lovers,* March 9, 1924.

MONROE, HARRIET. *Poets and Their Art,* August 1, 1926. *The Spyglass,* pp. 121–125.

MONTAGUE, MARGARET PRESCOTT. *Up Eel River,* May 20, 1928.

MOORE, GEORGE, ed. *An Anthology of Pure Poetry,* April 19, 1925.

———. *Avowals,* February 13, 1927.

———. *Celibate Lives,* September 18, 1927.

MOORE, MERRILL. *The Noise That Time Makes,* October 27, 1929.

MOORE, VIRGINIA. *Not Poppy,* May 30, 1926.

MOULT, THOMAS, ed. *The Best Poems of 1928,* December 30, 1928.

MUMFORD, LEWIS, ALFRED KREYMBORG, and PAUL ROSENFELD, eds. *The Second American Caravan,* November 11, 1928. *The Spyglass,* pp. 161–163.

MUNSON, GORHAM B. *Robert Frost: A Study in Sensibility and Common Sense,* November 27, 1927.

———. *Style and Form in American Prose,* September 8, 1929.

NASON, LEONARD. *Three Lights From a Match,* May 22, 1927.

NEUMANN, ALFRED. *The Devil,* August 26, 1928.

NEWMAN, FRANCES. *Dead Lovers Are Faithful Lovers,* May 13, 1928. *The Spyglass,* pp. 26–29.

———. *The Hard-Boiled Virgin,* December 19, 1926.

NICHOLSON, MEREDITH. *The Cavalier of Tennessee,* July 22, 1928. *The Spyglass,* pp. 79–82.

NICOLSON, HAROLD. *Some People,* October 2, 1927.

NIESE, RICHARD BEALL. *The Newspaper and Religious Publicity,* June 7, 1925.

NILES, BLAIR. *Condemned to Devil's Island,* June 3, 1928.

NILES, JOHN J. *Singing Soldiers,* April 7, 1927.

NOTCH, FRANK K. *King Mob,* July 13, 1930.

ODUM, HOWARD W. *Rainbow Round My Shoulder,* May 20, 1928.

O'FLAHERTY, LIAM. *Spring Sowing,* July 18, 1926.

OLIVER, EDITH. *The Love-Child,* September 11, 1927.

OLIVER, JOHN RATHBONE. *Victim and Victor,* July 7, 1929.

OMAN, CAROLA. *Crouchback,* December 22, 1929.

OSBORN, HENRY FAIRFIELD. *The Earth Speaks to Bryan,* August 30, 1925.

OSBORNE, LLOYD. *An Intimate Portrait of R.L.S.,* July 20, 1924.

O'SHEA, M. V., ed. *The Child: His Nature and His Needs,* September 7, 1924.

OSSENDOWSKI, FERDINAND. *Man and Mystery in Asia,* March 30, 1924.

OWSLEY, FRANK LAWRENCE. *State Rights in the Confederacy,* December 20, 1925. *The Spyglass,* pp. 197–200.

PAINE, RALPH D. *Four Bells,* March 16, 1924.

PALEN, LEWIS STANTON. *The White Devil of the Black Sea,* June 15, 1924.

PARRINGTON, VERNON LOUIS. *Main Currents in American Thought,* June 19, 1927. *The Spyglass,* pp. 131–137.

———. *Main Currents in American Thought,* volume III, November 24, 1930.

PARRISH, ANNE. *The Perennial Bachelor,* September 6, 1925.

PATERSON, ISABEL. *The Road of the Gods,* April 20, 1930.

PECK, WALTER EDWIN. *Shelley, His Life and Work,* February 5, 1928.

PETERKIN, JULIA. *Black April,* April 3, 1927. *The Spyglass,* pp. 20–23.

————. *Scarlet Sister Mary*, July 7, 1929.

PETTIT, E. *Moreover*, October 2, 1927.

PHILLIPS, ULRICH B. *Life and Labor in the Old South*, June 9, 1929. *The Spyglass*, pp. 211–217.

PINCKNEY, JOSEPHINE. *Sea-Drinking Cities*, January 15, 1928. *The Spyglass*, pp. 111–113.

PIPER, EDWIN FORD. *Barbed Wire and Wayfarers*, March 23, 1924.

RANLETT, LOUIS FELIX. *Let's Go!*, October 16, 1927.

RANSOM, JOHN CROWE. *Chills and Fever*, August 31, 1924.

RAUCAT, THOMAS. *The Honorable Picnic*, July 31, 1927.

READ, HERBERT. *Phases of English Poetry*, May 26, 1929.

REMARQUE, ERICH MARIA. *All Quiet on the Western Front*, June 16, 1929.

RICE, CALE YOUNG. *Bitter Brew*, May 17, 1925.

————. *Selected Plays and Poems*, March 6, 1927.

RICHARDS, LAURA E. *Captain January*, November 4, 1924.

RIDGE, LOLA. *Firehead*, January 12, 1930.

RIDING, LAURA. *The Close Chaplet*, August 7, 1927.

RITTENHOUSE, JESSIE B. *The Third Book of Modern Verse*, November 27, 1927.

ROBERTS, ELIZABETH MADOX. *Jingling in the Wind*, November 4, 1928.

————. *My Heart and My Flesh*, November 13, 1927.

————. *The Great Meadow*, March 16, 1930. *The Spyglass*, pp. 44–48.

————. *The Time of Man*, September 5, 1926. *The Spyglass*, pp. 16–20.

————. *Under the Tree*, November 16, 1930.

ROBESON, ESLANDA GOODE. *Paul Robeson: Negro*, July 20, 1930.

ROBINSON, EDWARD ARLINGTON. *Cavender's House*, May 26, 1929.

————. *Sonnets 1889–1927*, December 30, 1928.

————. *Tristram*, June 26, 1927.

ROGERS, WILL. *Letters of a Self-Made Diplomat*, November 21, 1926.

ROOSEVELT, THEODORE, JR., *Rank and File: True Stories of the Great War*, June 10, 1928.

RUSSELL, BERTRAND. *Education and the Good Life,* July 25, 1926.

RUTLEDGE, ARCHIBALD. *Days Off in Dixie,* July 13, 1924.

SALE, JOHN B. *The Tree Named John,* September 22, 1929.

SANDBURG, CARL. *Good Morning, America,* December 2, 1928. *The Spyglass,* pp. 114–115.

SASSOON, SIEGFRIED. *Memoirs of An Infantry Officer,* October 12, 1930. *The Spyglass,* pp. 188–193.

SAXON, LYLE. *Father Mississippi,* November 20, 1927.

SCHNITZLER, ARTHUR. *Rhapsody, A Dream Novel (Traum-novelle),* May 29, 1927.

SCOTT, EVELYN. *Migrations,* April 17, 1927.

——. *The Wave,* July 28, 1929.

SEIFFERT, MARJORIE ALLEN. *Ballads of the Singing Bowl,* June 5, 1927.

SHANNON, A. H. *The Negro in Washington,* July 20, 1930.

SHAPLEY, HARLOW. *Starlight,* January 23, 1927.

SHAW, GEORGE BERNARD. *The Intelligent Woman's Guide to Socialism and Capitalism,* August 12, 1928.

SHERMAN, STUART. *Critical Woodcuts,* May 9, 1926.

SIRINGO, CHARLES A. *Riata and Spurs,* June 5, 1927.

SITWELL, OSBERT. *England Reclaimed,* April 15, 1928.

SOLANO, SOLITA. *The Uncertain Feast,* October 19, 1924.

SPAETH, SIGMUND. *The Common Sense of Music,* August 10, 1924.

STALLINGS, LAURENCE. *Plumes,* October 12, 1924.

STEVENSON, ROBERT LOUIS. *The Works of Robert Louis Stevenson, South Seas Edition,* November 29, 1925.

STONEY, SAMUEL GAILLARD, and GERTRUDE MATHEWS SHELBY. *Black Genesis,* June 1, 1930.

STRACHEY, LYTTON. *Elizabeth and Essex: A Tragic History,* December 16, 1926.

STREETER, DANIEL W. *Camels,* November 6, 1927.

STRIBLING, T. S. *Bright Metal,* September 30, 1928.

——. *Teeftallow,* April 18, 1926. *The Spyglass,* pp. 11–16.

TARKINGTON, BOOTH. *Claire Ambler,* January 22, 1928. *The Spyglass,* pp. 75–79.

——. *The Plutocrat,* January 23, 1927.

TATE, ALLEN. *Mr. Pope and Other Poems,* February 10, 1929.
———. *Stonewall Jackson: The Good Soldier,* April 29, 1928.
The Spyglass, pp. 201–206.
TAYLOR, HENRY HAMMOND. *Knowing, Collecting and Restoring Early American Furniture,* May 18, 1930. *The Spyglass,* pp. 180–183.
TEASDALE, SARA. *Dark of the Moon,* October 17, 1926.
TERHUNE, ALBERT PAYSON. *Treve,* February 24, 1924.
THOMASON, JOHN W. *Fix Bayonets,* May 2, 1926.
———. *Red Pants,* May 29, 1927.
THOMPSON, DOROTHY. *The New Russia,* October 28, 1928.
THORNDIKE, RUSSELL, and REGINALD ARKELL. *The Tragedy of Mr. Punch,* November 16, 1924.
THURBER, JAMES, and E. B. WHITE. *Is Sex Necessary?,* November 10, 1929.
TRADER HORN (Alfred Aloysius Horn), *Harold the Webbed of the Young Vykings,* June 10, 1928.
UNTERMEYER, LOUIS. *The Forms of Poetry,* August 8, 1926.
VAN DOREN, CARL and MARK. *American and British Literature Since 1890,* September 27, 1925.
VAN DOREN, MARK. *Spring Thunder,* February 20, 1927.
VAN VECHTEN, CARL. *Nigger Heaven,* August 29, 1926.
———. *The Tattooed Countess,* October 5, 1924.
VANCE, JAMES I. *God's Open,* June 8, 1924.
VINAL, HAROLD. *Nor Youth Nor Age.* August 9, 1925.
WALPOLE, HUGH. *Harmer John,* December 26, 1926.
WALTON, EDA LOU. *The City Day: An Anthology of Recent American Poetry,* August 25, 1929.
WARREN, ROBERT PENN. *John Brown: The Making of a Martyr,* February 9, 1930.
WASSERMANN, JACOB. *Casper Hauser,* October 21, 1928.
WASSON, BEN. *The Devil Beats His Wife,* April 14, 1929.
WELLS, H. G. *Story of a Great Schoolmaster,* February 17, 1924.
———. *The Autocracy of Mr. Parham,* July 27, 1930.
———. *The Open Conspiracy,* October 7, 1928.
———. *The World of William Clissold,* December 12, 1926.

Wescott, Glenway. *The Apple of the Eye,* December 21, 1924. *The Spyglass,* pp. 59–60.
———. *The Grandmothers,* September 4, 1927.
West, Rebecca, ed. *Selected Poems of Carl Sandburg,* October 3, 1926.
Wharton, Edith. *The Children,* September 23, 1928. *The Spyglass,* pp. 83–87.
Wilkinson, Marguerite. *New Voices, An Introduction to Contemporary Poetry,* April 22, 1928.
Williams, Samuel Cole, ed. *Adair's History of the American Indians,* May 18, 1930.
———, ed. *Early Travels in the Tennessee Country, 1540–1800,* August 5, 1928.
Wills, Ridley. *Harvey Landrum,* November 23, 1924.
Wilson, Carter Godwin. *The Rural Negro,* July 20, 1930.
Winton, G. B. *Mexico: Past and Present,* May 20, 1928.
Wolfe, Thomas. *Look Homeward Angel,* February 16, 1930. *The Spyglass,* pp. 40–44.
Woodward, W. E. *Meet General Grant,* November 25, 1928.
Wyche, Cyril. *Outline of the Bible,* March 16, 1924.
Wylie, Elinor. *Angels and Earthly Creatures,* April 28, 1929. *The Spyglass,* pp. 115–117.
Yearbook of the Poetry Society of South Carolina, 1923, February 10, 1924.
Yeats, William Butler. *Autobiographies,* vol. 6 (*Reveries* and *The Trembling of the Veil*), Yeats's Collected Works, March 27, 1927.
———. *The Tower,* July 15, 1928.
Yeats-Brown, F. *The Lives of a Bengal Lancer,* November 16, 1930.
Young, Gordon. *Seibert of the Island,* August 23, 1925.
Young, Stark. *River House,* October 6, 1929. *The Spyglass,* pp. 34–39.
———. *The Street of the Islands,* October 26, 1930.
Zweig, Arnold. *The Case of Sergeant Grischa,* December 23, 1928.

VII. *Miscellanea*

"A Symposium: The Agrarians Today," *Shenandoah,* III (Summer, 1952), 14–33. [Seven of the contributors to *I'll Take My Stand* answer questions submitted by the editors; Davidson's replies on pages 16–22.]

"Decentralization: The Outlook for 1941, A Symposium of Opinion," *Free America,* V (January, 1941), 10–16. [Davidson's contribution on pages 11–12.]

"On Teaching Democracy Through Literature." A Paper Read at the Conference on "Zeal for American Democracy" of the Nashville Public Schools. At Howard School, February 18, 1949. [Mimeographed, nine pages.]

Singin' Billy. An Opera in Two Acts. Drama and Lyrics by Donald Davidson. Music by Charles Faulkner Bryan. First produced at Vanderbilt University Theatre, Nashville, Tennessee, April 23–28, 1952, under the joint sponsorship of the Department of Music of George Peabody College for Teachers and Vanderbilt University Theatre. [Unpublished, except in mimeographed form for theatrical production.]

"The Agrarian South: An Interpretation." Synopsis and subsequent discussion of a paper read at the Second Annual meeting of the Southern Historical Association, Vanderbilt University, November 20, 1936, *Journal of Southern History,* III (February, 1937), 83–85.

The Fugitive. 4 volumes, April, 1922—December, 1925. Nashville: Fugitive Publishing Company. Edited in rotation by Davidson, John Crowe Ransom, Allen Tate, and other members of the Fugitive group.

"The Inversive Method of Narration in the Novels and Stories of Joseph Conrad." [Unpublished M.A. thesis, Vanderbilt University, 1922.]

"The Old—or New—Tennessee River Finally Subdued," Nashville *Tennessean TVA Jubilee Edition,* October 2, 1949, p. 54. [Excerpts from Davidson's two volume history *The Tennessee.*]

VIII. *Biographical and Critical Material*

ALLEN, CHARLES. "The Fugitive," *South Atlantic Quarterly,* XLIII (October, 1944), 382–389. [A brief survey of the *Fugitive* magazine, its origin and purpose.]

AUERBACH, M. MORTON. "Conservatism and its Contemporary American Advocates." Unpublished Ph.D. dissertation, Columbia University, 1958. [A history and critique of modern conservative theory containing a section on the Vanderbilt Agrarians (pages 123–152).]

BEATTY, RICHMOND CROOM. "Donald Davidson as Fugitive-Agrarian," *Hopkins Review,* V (Winter, 1952), 12–27. LOUIS D. RUBIN, JR., and ROBERT D. JACOBS, eds., *Southern Renascence* (Baltimore: Johns Hopkins Press, 1953), pp. 392–412. [Examines the central concerns of Davidson's prose and poetry.]

————. "Fugitive and Agrarian Writers at Vanderbilt," *Tennessee Historical Quarterly,* III (March, 1924), 3–23. Condensed as "By Way of Background," RICHMOND CROOM BEATTY, ed., *A Vanderbilt Miscellany, 1919–1944* (Nashville: Vanderbilt University Press, 1944), pp. 11–27. [Davidson's views on modern poetry are summarized in the original article (pages 9–10), but this section is omitted in the condensation.]

————, FLOYD C. WATKINS, and THOMAS DANIEL YOUNG, eds., *The Literature of the South* (Chicago: Scott, Foresman and Company, 1952), pp. 766–767. [Contains a biographical note introducing selections from Davidson's work.]

Bowen, Frances Jean. *"The New Orleans Double Dealer:* 1921–May, 1926, A Critical History." Unpublished Ph.D. dissertation, Vanderbilt University, 1954. [Contains a biographical note and reproduces two poems contributed by Davidson to the *Double Dealer* (pages 272–274).]

Bowling, Lawrence E. "An Analysis of Davidson's 'Lee in the Mountains'," *Georgia Review,* VI (Spring, 1952), 69–88. [A thorough historical explication of the poem.]

Bradbury, John M. *Renaissance in the South, A Critical History of the Literature, 1920–1960* (Chapel Hill: The University of North Carolina, 1963), p. 29. [Davidson's poetry is briefly characterized.]

———. *The Fugitives, A Critical Account* (Chapel Hill: The University of North Carolina Press, 1958). [A primarily critical assessment, with little researched historical content, of the contributions of the major Fugitives and related writers to literature. Davidson's criticism and poetry are discussed (pages 24–26, 68–74, 263–265, and *passim*).]

Cater, Catherine. "Four Voices Out of the South," *Michigan Alumnus Quarterly Review,* L (Winter, 1944), 168–173. [Analyzes the relationships between Southern Agrarianism and the poetry of Davidson (pages 168–169), Tate, Warren, and Ransom.]

Connelly, Thomas Lawrence. "The Vanderbilt Agrarians: Time and Place in Southern Tradition," *Tennessee Historical Quarterly,* XXII (March, 1963), 22–37. [Examines the importance of the Agrarian movement within a historical context.]

Cowan, Louise. "Donald Davidson: The 'Long Street'," William E. Walker and Robert L. Welker, eds., *Reality and Myth, Essays in American Literature in Memory of Richmond Croom Beatty* (Nashville: Vanderbilt University Press, 1964), pp. 98–116. [The importance of tradition as a theme in Davidson's poetry is analyzed.]

———. "The Communal World of Southern Literature," *Georgia Review,* XIV (Fall, 1960), 248–257. [Surveys the nature and themes of modern Southern writing and discusses Davidson's poems "Aunt Maria and the Gourds" and "Georgia Pastorals" (pages 255–256).]

———. *The Fugitive Group, A Literary History* (Baton Rouge: Louisiana State University Press, 1959). [A carefully researched and authoritative history of the *Fugitive* magazine and the intellectual milieu of the collaboration which produced it; emphasizes Davidson's position as a cohesive force in the group.]

———. "The *Pietas* of Southern Poetry," Louis D. Rubin, Jr., and Robert D. Jacobs, eds., *South: Modern Southern Literature in Its Cultural Setting* (Garden City: Dolphin Books, Doubleday and Company, 1961), pp. 95–114. [Distinguishes Southern poetry from contemporary national poetry of the 1920s and 1930s; Davidson's poem, "Lines Written for Allen Tate on His Sixtieth Anniversary," is analyzed (pages 95–98).]

Daniel, Robert. "The Critics of Nashville," *Tennessee Studies in Literature*, I (1956), 19–26. [A Survey of the importance of the Fugitive group as critics.]

Daniels, Jonathan. *A Southerner Discovers the South* (New York: The Macmillan Company, 1938), pp. 111–119. [A Southern journalist reports on his visit with Davidson to talk about Agrarianism in chapter 13, "Night in Nashville."]

Davis, Louise. "He Clings to Enduring Values," Nashville *Tennessean Magazine*, September 4, 1949, pp. 6–8. [An informal personality sketch with substantial biographical content.]

Drake, Robert. "Donald Davidson and the Ancient Mariner," *Vanderbilt Alumnus*, XLIX (January–February, 1964), 18–22. [An informal essay by a former student recording his personal impressions of Davidson.]

Emerson, O.B. "Prophet Next Door," William E. Walker and Robert L. Welker, eds., *Reality and Myth, Essays in American Literature in Memory of Richmond Croom Beatty* (Nashville: Vanderbilt University Press, 1964), pp. 237–274. [Discusses Davidson's early influence on the literary reputation of William Faulkner (pages 240–243, 258, 272–273).]

England, Kenneth. "They Came Home Again: Fugitives Return," *Georgia Review,* XIV (Spring, 1960), 80–89. [On the significance of the 1956 reunion of the Fugitives at Vanderbilt University.]

ETHRIDGE, JAMES M., ed. *Contemporary Authors, A Bio-Bibliographical Guide to the Current Authors and Their Works,* volume 7–8 (Detroit: Gale Research Company, 1963), pp. 124–125. [A biographical outline of Davidson's life and career with a substantial bibliography.]

FAIN, JOHN TYREE. "Introduction," Donald Davidson, *The Spyglass, Views and Reviews, 1924–1930* (Nashville: Vanderbilt University Press, 1963), pp. v-xviii. [A historical sketch of Davidson's years as editor of the book page of the Nashville Tennessean, 1924–1930. Fain also provides a brief biographical sketch (p. xxi).]

FLETCHER, JOHN GOULD. *Life is My Song, The Autobiography of John Gould Fletcher* (New York: Farrar and Rinehart, 1937). [Fletcher records his impressions after a visit with Davidson and Ransom at Vanderbilt in 1927 (pages 338–344).]

———. "The Modern Southern Poets," *Westminster Magazine,* XXIII (Winter, 1935), 229–251. [The portion devoted to Davidson (pages 233–236) is an enthusiastic appraisal of his poetic achievement.]

FREEZE, LESLIE H. "The Poetry of Donald Davidson." Unpublished M. A. thesis, University of Kansas, 1964. [Examines some of Davidson's attitudes toward life and literature as reflected in his poetry.]

GORLIER, CLAUDIO. "Il Sud di un «Reazionario»: Donald Davidson," *Questioni,* Anno VIII (January–March, 1960), 52–55. [An appreciation by an Italian.]

HARKNESS, DAVID J. *Tennessee in Literature,* The University of Tennessee News Letter, volume XXVIII, November, 1949. [A pamphlet which quotes Davidson on biographical details (pages 21–23).]

HARTSOCK, ERNEST. "Roses in the Desert: A View of Contemporary Southern Verse," *Sewanee Review,* XXXVII (July, 1929), 328–335. [A brief paragraph is devoted to Davidson's achievement and promise as a poet and critic (page 333).]

HERZBERG, MAX J. *The Reader's Encyclopedia of American Lit-*

erature (New York: Thomas Y. Crowell Company, 1962). [Contains a brief entry on Davidson's career and reputation (page 238).]

HOFFMAN, FREDERICK J., CHARLES ALLEN, and CAROLYN ULRICH. *The Little Magazine, A History and a Bibliography* (Princeton: Princeton University Press, 1946). [Includes a historical account of the *Fugitive* magazine and Davidson's importance to the endeavor (pages 116–124). The bibliography is helpful in identifying other little magazines to which Davidson contributed.]

HOLLAND, ROBERT B. "The Agrarian Manifesto: A Generation Later," *Mississippi Quarterly*, X (Spring, 1957), 73–78. [A summary essay on the meaning of *I'll Take My Stand*.]

HOLMAN, C. HUGH. "Literature and Culture: The *Fugitive*-Agrarians," *Social Forces*, XXXVII (October, 1958), 15–19. [The Fugitive-Agrarian movement viewed as a response to social and cultural change.]

IRISH, MARION D. "Proposed Roads to the New South, 1941: Chapel Hill Planners vs. Nashville Agrarians," *Sewanee Review*, XLIX (January–March, 1941), 1–27. [Davidson is briefly mentioned as an Agrarian philosopher.]

JONES, HOWARD MUMFORD. "Is There a Southern Renaissance?", *Virginia Quarterly Review*, VI (April, 1930), 184–197. [In a survey of contemporary Southern literature, Davidson is commended for his book reviewing.]

KREYMBORG, ALFRED. *Our Singing Strength, An Outline of American Poetry (1620–1930)* (New York: Coward-McCann, 1929). [Davidson's poetry is briefly criticized (pages 564–565).]

KUNITZ, STANLEY J., and HOWARD HAYCRAFT, eds. *Twentieth Century Authors* (New York: The H. W. Wilson Company, 1942). [Quotes Davidson on biographical facts (pages 350–351).]

———, and VINETA COLBY, eds. *Twentieth Century Authors, First Supplement* (New York: The H. W. Wilson Company, 1955). [Additional information on literary activities (page 263).]

Millet, Fred B. *Contemporary American Authors, A Critical Survey and 219 Bio-Bibliographies* (New York: Harcourt, Brace and Company, 1940). [Contains a biographical sketch with a bibliography (pages 311–312) and a brief critical comment on Davidson's poetry (page 147).]

Mims, Edwin. *History of Vanderbilt University* (Nashville: Vanderbilt University Press, 1946). [Discusses Davidson's part in the development of the English department and graduate studies at Vanderbilt (pages 411–417).]

Norred, Charlotte Evelyn. "Regionalism Vs. Metropolitanism in 1929: A Study in Critical Attitudes." Unpublished M. A. thesis, Vanderbilt University, 1939. [A summary of regional differences in critical attitudes as expressed in 1929 in Davidson's reviews for his book page in the Nashville *Tennessean* and reviews in the New York *Times Book Review* and the *Saturday Review of Literature*.]

O'Connor, William Van. *Sense and Sensibility in Modern Poetry* (Chicago: University of Chicago Press, 1948). [The regional themes of Davidson's poetry are briefly mentioned (page 203).]

Parks, Edd Winfield. *Southern Poets, Representative Selections* (New York: American Book Company, 1936). [In his critical introduction, Parks discusses the work of Davidson (pages cxxiv–cxxvii).]

Pressly, T. J. "Agrarianism: An Autopsy; Appraisal of the Nashville Agrarian Movement," *Sewanee Review*, XLIX April–June, 1941), 145–163. [A general survey of the Agrarian movement with special attention to the contributors to *I'll Take My Stand*.]

Purdy, Rob Roy, ed. *Fugitives' Reunion, Conversations at Vanderbilt May 3–5, 1956* (Nashville: Vanderbilt University Press, 1959). [Transcripts of recorded conversations in which Davidson participated among the Fugitive writers on the occasion of their reunion.]

Rock, Virginia. "The Making and Meaning of *I'll Take My Stand*: A Study in Utopian-Conservatism, 1925–1939." Unpublished Ph.D. dissertation, University of Minnesota, 1961.

[A study of the backgrounds and genesis of the *I'll Take My Stand* symposium, its repercussions, and a critique of its meaning. Among the appendices is a biographical essay on Davidson (pages 474–484).]

———. "The Twelve Southerners: Biographical Essays," Twelve Southerners, *I'll Take My Stand, The South and the Agrarian Tradition,* Harper Torchbooks, The Academy Library (New York: Harper and Brothers, 1962), pp. 360–385. [A brief biographical and critical estimate of Davidson's career is provided (pages 363–365).]

ROSSITER, CLINTON. *Conservatism in America* (New York: Alfred A. Knopf, 1955). Second Edition, Revised (New York: Vintage Books, 1962). [In the first edition Davidson is mentioned once as a contributor to *I'll Take My Stand* (page 206), but in the revised edition he is characterized as "the ranking agrarian still left in the South" (pages 229–231).]

RUBIN, LOUIS D., JR. "The Concept of Nature in Modern Southern Poetry," *American Quarterly,* IX (Spring, 1957), 63–71. [Discusses concepts of nature as reflected in Davidson's poetry (pages 65–67).]

———. *The Faraway Country, Writers of the Modern South* (Seattle: University of Washington Press, 1963). [In a chapter on "The Poetry of Agrarianism," the Agrarian themes in Davidson's poetry are analyzed (pages 161–165).]

STEWART, JOHN LINCOLN. *The Burden of Time: The Fugitives and Agrarians* (Princeton: Princeton University Press, 1965). [An extensive revision of Stewart's doctoral dissertation.]

———. "The Fugitive-Agrarian Writers: A History and a Criticism." Unpublished Ph.D. dissertation, Ohio State University, 1947. [Examines the achievement and influence of the major Fugitive-Agrarian writers in American literature. Davidson's work is analyzed in the following sections: Chapter III, Section 7, "Davidson's Poetry During the Period of the *Fugitive,*" pages 128–139; Chapter V, Section 4, "Davidson and the Old South: The Tall men," pages 266–275; Chapter VI, Section 6, "Agrarianism and Davidson's Studies in Regionalism," pages 345–349; Chapter VII, Section 1, "The

Poetry of Ransom and Davidson in the Period of Agrarianism," pages 359–364.]

STEWART, RANDALL. *American Literature and Christian Doctrine* (Baton Rouge: Louisiana State University Press, 1958). [Suggests that "Lee in the Mountains" displays the persistence of a Puritan influence in modern Southern literature (pages 20–21).]

————. "Donald Davidson," LOUIS D. RUBIN, JR., and ROBERT D. JACOBS, eds. *South: Modern Southern Literature in its Cultural Setting* (Garden City: Dolphin Books, Doubleday and Company, 1961), pp. 248–259. [A general critical estimate of Davidson's prose and poetry.]

STUART, JESSE. *Beyond Dark Hills, A Personal Story* (New York: E. P. Dutton and Company, 1938). [Stuart relates in chapter IX (pages 281–327) his experiences at Vanderbilt University where he encountered Davidson, the teacher who first encouraged him to become a writer. Davidson is also mentioned in a number of the sonnets composing Stuart's *Man With a Bull-Tongue Plow* (New York: E. P. Dutton and Company, 1934; revised edition, 1959).]

TATE, ALLEN. *Sixty American Poets 1896–1944* (Washington: The Library of Congress, 1945; revised edition, 1954). [Contains a preliminary check list of Davidson's works with a critical note by Tate (pages 28–29; revised edition, pages 21–22.]

THORP, WILLARD. *American Writing in the Twentieth Century* (Cambridge: Harvard University Press, 1960). [Comments briefly on the nature and subject matter of Davidson's writings (pages 243–244).]

UNTERMEYER, LOUIS, ed. *Modern American Poetry, A Critical Anthology,* Third Revised Edition (New York: Harcourt Brace and Company, 1925). [As an introduction to selections from Davidson's verse, Untermeyer includes a biographical and critical note (pages 356–357) which was revised and expanded in the following subsequent editions: Fourth (1930), pages 675–677; Fifth (1936), pages 514–515; Sixth (1942), pages 537–538.]

WARREN, ROBERT PENN. "A Note on Three Southern Poets,"
    Poetry, XL (May, 1932), 103–113. [A critical essay on the
    verse of Fletcher, Davidson (pages 108–110), and Ransom.]
WELLS, HENRY W. *Poet and Psychiatrist Merrill Moore, M. D.*
    (New York: Twayne Publishers, 1955). [Considers David-
    son's influence on the work of Merrill Moore and briefly
    criticizes his poetry (pages 51–52).]